TRINITY AND TRUTH

The Story of Atonement

The Story of Atonement

oooooooooo

STEPHEN SYKES

For god was in Christ, and made agrement bitwene the worlde and hym sylfe and imputed not their synnes unto them: and hath committed to us the preachynge of the atonement.

(2 Corinthians 5:19, William Tyndale's translation, 1526)

DARTON · LONGMAN + TODD

First published in 1997 by
Darton, Longman and Todd Ltd
1 Spencer Court
140–142 Wandsworth High Street
London SW18 4JJ

ISBN 0–232–52213–8

A catalogue record for this book is available from the British Library

The Scripture quotations used are, unless otherwise indicated, from the
Revised English Bible, copyright © Oxford University Press and Cambridge
University Press 1989.

Designed by Sandie Boccacci
Phototypeset in 10¾/13½ pt Baskerville by Intype London Ltd
Printed and bound in Great Britain by
Page Bros, Norwich

Dedicated with affection
to my sisters and brothers in
the sacred ministry in the
Diocese of Ely.

CONTENTS

ooooooooooo

Contents

FOREWORD

ooooooooooo

Trinity and Truth is a series of theological books written
by authors convinced that there is truth to be spoken
about God, and that such truth is best explored when we
speak about God as Father, Son and Holy Spirit.

Such a claim for truth has always been controversial. In
the Fourth Gospel's account of his trial before Pilate, Jesus
said, 'All who are not deaf to truth listen to my voice'.
Pilate's famous reply, 'What is truth?' was neither jest nor
invitation to philosophical debate. It was an expression of
impatient dissent. He intended to be understood as the
sole arbiter of truth, because his was (he believed) the
dominant ideology. And to illustrate how feeble were
the claims of the 'king of the Jews', whose invisible
'kingdom' seemed to be on the point of collapse, Pilate
had Jesus flogged.

Pilate's question has a post-modern ring about it. The
truth for him was the extent to which he could impose his
power over Jesus, and everyone else within range of
his voice. But, said the writer of the Fourth Gospel, this
mockery of a judicial process contained a reversal of
appearances. It is the judge who is judged. The prince
of this world turns out to be powerless. There is another
truth, which is a way, which leads to life.

In the long and turbulent history of Christian theology
it has often been forgotten that belief in the Trinity entails

ix

a way of life. To many the doctrine of the Trinity has seemed too erudite to be relevant; and in truth theologians have not always avoided a self-defeating level of detailed pseudo-precision. But the fearsome complexities of the classic disputes of the early centuries are not the main concern of this series. The authors intend, instead, to demonstrate Trinitarian theology at work in the exploration and elucidation of modern questions.

Augustine of Hippo once pointed out that merely to utter the names, Father, Son and Holy Spirit is physically to separate the sounds in time, and so to be misleading about the unity of 'substance' or 'being' of the three; for there is an irreplaceable history or narrative attaching to each of these names. And so what we signify when we utter the simple word 'God', is rich, complex and full of resource.

It is the purpose of this series to draw upon the continuing resourcefulness of Trinitarian theology. The books will not be restricted to expositions of classic doctrines, but will concern every aspect of Christian life, worship and spirituality. Ancient orthodoxy was never intended to be a static, backward-looking set of intellectual constraints. It is the belief of the authors of this series that the Trinitarian traditions of the Church are subversive and liberating convictions founded upon a willingness to listen freshly to the voice of truth.

Stephen Ely

PREFACE

ooooooooooo

The atonement, God making peace between himself and humankind, has been written about in many different ways. There are studies of the doctrine of the atonement in the New Testament, taking each book or group of books separately and giving an account of its contents. There are histories of the doctrine of the atonement from the earliest times to the present day. There are philosophical or doctrinal analyses of theories of the atonement, attempting to account for the necessity of the astonishing means by which God has made reconciliation. It would be presumptuous to say that this work is completely unlike all previous such undertakings. But, in truth, it is a little different.

I have tried to get inside, as it were, the way in which Christians inhabit the atonement. In my view, they live in the story of the atonement. As the seventeenth-century hymn-writer put it:

> Here might I stay and sing
> no story so divine.

Had it been more readily intelligible, I would gladly have chosen 'No Story So Divine' as the title of this book. But this story exists in our heads in snatches. Part of my argument is that it is not really possible to write a continuous, single-line narrative detailing God's motives and actions

from beginning to end, without falling into serious doctrinal difficulties. So we allow the story to exist in different
versions, and we keep parts of it in our head in rather
different ways.

We have, then, a kind of outline in mind of the way in
which God has made peace with humankind, and we allow
our encounters with the Bible to illuminate that outline
in snatches. Very important, of course, are the stories of
Jesus: not just the passion narrative, but also many other
parts of the Gospel, illuminate atonement. So I have
allowed myself the liberty of using the Scriptures the way
(I believe) most Christians, including Christian preachers,
use them.

The reader will not find an outline of 'St Paul's understanding of atonement', followed by those of the gospel
writers and the author of the letter to Hebrews. I am not
unfamiliar with the differences between the sources. But
the way we live with differences has everything to do with
our first inhabiting the story, and then responding to
various emphases which emerge from our reading of the
texts. As a consequence, this book has been written quite
close to the Scriptures, and in that sense I hope it will be
accessible to all ordinary readers of them, whether they
see themselves as theologically learned or not.

This book began as a series of workshops with the clergy
of the Diocese of Ely. Our discussions helped to develop
and change my thinking on a number of topics. In the
midst of revising the manuscript, I paid my first visit to
the Holy Land. This experience, too, had a major impact
on the way I read the Bible, especially the gospels. No one
who sees the scale on which Herod the Great imposed
himself on the landscape, to the impoverishment of the
people, will ever read Jesus' references to tax and indebtedness in the same way again. But is that not typical? Does it
not inherently belong to the way in which we inhabit these

snatches of the story of atonement, that we are constantly surprised by the uncovering of new depths in them? My hope is that this exploration of some of the diverse ways in which we tell the story of atonement, and the questions we put to that story, will reveal to us some new facets of God's love for humanity, and give rise to new praise. 'This is my friend, in whose sweet praise I all my days could gladly spend.'

Let me express publicly my thanks: to my sisters and brothers who work with me in the sacred ministry of the Church of God in this place; to Bishop Alec Graham of Newcastle, Chairman of the Doctrine Commission of the Church of England, who read and commented on this manuscript; to my stimulating colleagues on that Commission who were composing *The Mystery of Salvation* as I was writing this book; to Dr Jonathan Knight, my research assistant, and Miss Sue Holgate, my secretary, for a lot of very hard work; and to my friends in Mawddach Crescent, Arthog, who are fun, encouraging and discreet in equal measure.

1

ooooooooo

What is Atonement?

I start with forgiveness, because that is within everyone's experience. Television has strangely reinforced the immediacy and urgency of forgiveness in our minds. Scarcely is the blood dry on the scene of a crime before some eager journalist has asked the victim or the victim's relative, 'Can you forgive whoever did this?' Some say they can; some say they cannot; some are so caught up in the confusion of the tragedy that they say nothing coherent. The question is manifestly unfair and insensitive, and occasionally, when the response is a blood-chilling cry for revenge, one feels that a new victim has been created. But the journalist's defence is public interest; and that is not without reason. We want to know whether forgiveness is possible.

An unforgettable image remains in my mind of a veteran of the second world war, a prisoner in the infamous camps of the Burma–Thailand railway. Interviewed on television on the fiftieth anniversary of peace in the East, he was finally asked the inevitable question, whether he had forgiven his Japanese torturers. It had been a week in which no one watching television or listening to the radio could have escaped hearing one reply or another. The old man sat in his chair before the cameras and his highly sophisticated interviewer. He had been fluent about his experiences in the camps, which were horrific. But now he paused. 'Well', he said, in gentle Geordie tones, 'I hope

1

the Japanese never do things like that again. I can't speak for everyone, but as for myself, I'm a Christian so I have to forgive.' And as if overwhelmed by what he had said, he raised his hands, index fingers aloft, got up from his chair and left the studio.

The Christian faith creates an expectation at least of the profession of forgiveness. This is public knowledge because of the explicit words of the Lord's Prayer – 'And forgive us our trespasses, as we forgive those who trespass against us' – and because of the example of Jesus during his own torture and crucifixion. Moreover every communicant Christian knows the sentence, based on words attributed to Jesus at the Last Supper, 'This is my blood of the new covenant, which is shed for you and for many for the forgiveness of sins'.[1] And another ancient liturgical text, with its roots in Scripture, says explicitly:

> 'O Lamb of God, that takest away
> the sins of the world, have mercy on us'.

Atonement is the forgiveness of sins by the shedding of the blood of Jesus. There is, then, a relationship of some kind between the death of Jesus (and not just the death, but the life, death, resurrection and ascension of Jesus) and the forgiveness of human sin. The etymology of 'atonement' is fascinating.[2] 'At one' has been an adverbial phrase in English since the early fourteenth century, meaning, as now, an existence in harmony or friendship. 'To one' was formerly used as a verb, signifying to make one or to unite. 'Onement' was used as a noun by Wycliffe in the fourteenth century. 'Atonement', for which there is evidence from the early sixteenth century, took the place of 'onement'. More (1478–1535) and Tyndale (1494–1536) used 'atonement', the latter to translate both Leviticus 23:28 (a reference to the Day of Atonement), and 2 Corinthians 5:18–19:

> Nevertheless all things are of God, which hath reconciled us with himself by Jesus Christ and hath given unto us the office to preach the atonement. For God was in Christ, and made agreement between the world and himself, and imputed not their sins unto them: and hath committed to us the preaching of the atonement.

From 1611 the King James 'Authorised' Version replaced 'atonement' with 'reconciliation'.[2]

At this point, the unwary reader must be warned that, despite the attractive simplicity of the English word 'atonement', there is nothing simple about the way in which atonement is explained, interpreted and discussed in Christian theology. Nor is this a case of modern intellectuals making life difficult for the simple Bible-believer. On the contrary, the complications begin in the Bible itself. The enquirer after an explanation of atonement in the New Testament would most likely be sent to Paul's letter to the Romans, or to the letter to the Hebrews. Both have formidable reputations for obscurity and complexity, and both have given rise to mountains of commentaries from very early days.

Consider a single chapter from the letter to the Romans – chapter 5, which deals pre-eminently with aspects of atonement. What is it about? To make matters clearer, commentators frequently offer their own titles by way of summary. In this case there has been an astonishing variety of different attempts, an indication of the density of the argument. Professor Charles Cranfield settles on 'A life characterised by peace with God'; the Revised English Bible offers 'Life in Christ'.[3] A recent Bible translation includes five subheadings:

- The Christian's hope (vv.1–5);
- Justification and reconciliation by Christ's sacrificial death (vv.6–11);

- Christ's reversal of Adam's wrongdoing, condemnation and death (vv.12–17);
- How righteousness and obedience overpower iniquity and disobedience (vv.18–19);
- How grace overcomes law and sin (vv.20–1).

On any showing, these subjects are among matters which must be explained if the atonement is to be interpreted. But the extent of the problem is indicated in that there are no fewer than six separate interpretations of a single Greek phrase ('inasmuch as all sinned', Romans 5:12, REB), which Cranfield discusses in seven closely argued pages.

Hebrews is, if anything, even more formidable to the modern reader, since it presupposes a considerable knowledge of the Old Testament priestly and sacrificial system. An entire section of the book – from chapter 5:11 to the end of chapter 10 – depends on an assertion that Jesus Christ was designated by God 'high priest in the order of Melchizedek.' Then follow the discouraging words:

> About Melchizedek we have much to say, much that is difficult to explain to you, now that you have proved so slow to learn. By this time you ought to be teachers, but instead you need someone to teach you the ABC of God's oracles over again (Rom. 5:11–12, REB).

Without considerable and repeated explanations, modern congregations are in no better case. Hebrews heavily predominates in the Epistle readings set for Holy Week, and one wonders what is made of them. In the early part of the last century, the exposition of Hebrews was carried out in churches at a semi-popular level, and with great intensity.[4] Jesus' perpetual priesthood, his being able to save those who approach God through him, his sacrifice of himself at the climax of history to abolish sin, his heavenly intercession on behalf of sinners – all these were doctrines carrying an intense emotional weight in the faith-experience of many ordinary Christian people. It is very doubtful how much of this inheritance remains. Hebrews strikes many people today not just as a complex and difficult work, but also as artificial and theoretical. For its message to carry conviction you apparently have first to believe that God intended the whole sacrificial system described in the Old Testament – a difficult exercise for the modern reader, who will have little natural sympathy for the thought that, 'without the shedding of blood there is no forgiveness' (Heb. 9:22).

Vital in carrying the message of atonement in the modern church is the language of the liturgy and hymns. We have been freed from the slavery of sin by Christ, the living Word; he gave or offered himself, once for all on the cross, for us and for our salvation; he put an end to death by dying for us and revealed the resurrection by rising to new life; he made a full atonement for the sins of the whole world by suffering death on the cross for our redemption; we receive the forgiveness of sin as among the benefits of Christ's passion; the Lamb of God takes away the sins of the world. All these phrases and sentences are the common coin of the Church's worship, and it is easy for practising Christians to treat them as self-explanatory. Even in preaching, complex-sounding abstractions like justification, redemption, sanctification, expiation, propitiation and reconciliation can with a little ingenuity be expanded by phrases, such as 'for us', 'on our behalf', 'for our sake', and so forth. But the explanations are not obvious, and if an enquirer without a religious background but with an instinct to be disputatious were to demand one, we might quickly be in some difficulty.

SOME THEORIES OF ATONEMENT

The Bible and the liturgy are not the only source of complexity in the interpretation of the atonement. This is, after all, the very heart of the faith. And as a result, virtually every theological teacher of any profundity has written on this subject, from the earliest days to the present. To study the doctrine of atonement in the history of Christian theology is a mountainous task. There are now even hillocks of histories of its history – indeed, the writing of historical monographs on the atonement has been something of a British and North American theological speciality from the nineteenth century onwards. We find ourselves well-served with literature which attempts to organise the vast quantity of scholarship from earlier generations.

As is so often the case with histories of complex arguments, it is a brief, and apparently clear and simple book that has made the profoundest impression on all subsequent discussion. In 1930 a Swedish Lutheran scholar (and later bishop), Gustav Aulén, wrote a book which claimed to summarise and classify the whole history of atonement theology into three main approaches: the classic, the Latin and the subjective or humanistic. The book was swiftly translated into English, and achieved a prominence out of all proportion to its size.[5]

Aulén's three groupings were not, however, of equal weight or importance, and the book contained an argument in favour of the classic understanding of atonement, from which its title, *Christus Victor*, derived. This presents atonement as the outcome of a battle, in which Christ fights against and triumphs over evil, to which humanity is in bondage. The way the battle is constructed contains a striking paradox: God is presented simultaneously as the reconciler (through the act of his Son), and also the One who is reconciled. God both offers the sacrifice in and through the Son, and also receives the sacrifice as the Father. Aulén fully understands the paradoxical character of this position, but holds that it is impossible to construct a rationally consistent doctrine or theory of atonement. He prefers to speak instead of the classic 'idea', 'motif' or 'theme'. He finds this view set out in the writings of Irenaeus (*c.* 130–200) and impressively revived by Martin Luther (1483–1546).

By contrast, the Latin type is a fully fledged theory, with a background in law, setting out the precise terms on which God receives due compensation for the injury done to his honour by human sin. The atonement is a work of satisfaction carried out by Christ, in his human nature, and offered to God. The medieval theologian, Anselm of Canterbury (1033–1109), gave outstanding expression to this theory, which was picked up and elaborated by the theologians of Protestant orthodoxy in the seventeenth century.

The last type, the so-called subjective or humanistic view, strongly emphasises God's benevolence, and criticises the idea that he could in any sense require the innocent suffering of the Son. Atonement happens, so the theory goes, through the spiritual enlightenment and moral persuasion of the believer, attracted and changed by the message of forgiveness. This view becomes prominent in the modern world, and there are many examples and variations of the theory.

From this brief summary of a relatively short book, it is at once clear how much variety is contained in the history of atonement theology. Aulén went to some trouble to distinguish between a theory and a motif, though his point has frequently been overlooked. He wrote as follows:

> I have tried to be consistent in speaking of the classic *idea*

of the Atonement, never of the, or a, theory or classic *theory*. I have reserved the word *theory*, and usually the word *doctrine*, for the Latin and the 'subjective' types. For the classic idea of the Atonement has never been put forward, like the other two, as a rounded and finished theological *doctrine*, it has always been an idea, a *motif*, a theme, expressed in many different variations . . . But it has never been shaped into a rational theory.[6]

Others added more theories. An influential Anglican, Oliver Quick, writing in 1939, adopted Aulén's groups but added a fourth, the sacrificial theory.[7] The Welsh theologian T.H. Hughes exhaustively surveyed modern atonement theology in seven separate categories, with brief accounts of no fewer than 42 British theologians of the nineteenth and twentieth centuries.[8] The sheer quantity and variety of the arguments began to shed doubt on the credibility of the whole enterprise.

In the 1950s reaction against theory construction set in. Instead of the dry enumeration of alternative rational constructs purporting to explain how Christ achieved human redemption, another writer (H.A. Hodges) focused instead on the complementary ways in which Christ acts as peace-maker and restorer. Christ cancels offences and restores personal relationship with God, he recreates corrupt human nature, he restores the priestly function of humanity, he delivers humanity from the power of Satan, and he breaks down the fear of self-knowledge which binds us to our sins.[9]

The movement away from theory is still stronger in F.W. Dillistone's *The Christian Understanding of Atonement* (1968). In a wide-ranging analysis, Dillistone accepted that all Christian witness to the saving effect of the death and resurrection of Christ is theory-laden. None the less he does not believe that the atonement can be understood by means of a series of theories for comparison and criticism. Atonement implies restoration of damage or disruption. This can be discerned on four levels – those of the universe as a whole, of a total society (tribe, city, nation or state), of the kin-group (family, friends) and of the self. In respect of each of these four levels we can see in the Christian tradition a combination of analogues and parables. The analogues are what Dillistone terms 'patterns of corporate experience', and the parables 'examples of individual achievement'. In each of these various ways there is set up 'an imaginative pattern of comparison', linking the death and resurrection of Christ with the wider experiences of humanity.[10] The structure turns out as follows:

Humanity in relation to:	Analogue	Parable
Universe	Sacrifice	Redemption
Society	Tragedy	Judgement
Kin-group	Compassion	Forgiveness
Self	Perfect integration	Word of reconciliation

He is not concerned to produce a theory or theories from this analysis. None of the patterns of comparison is dispensable from a full interpretation of atonement. A rich and suggestive treasury of ideas is presented for exploration, working on a variety of levels.

We have moved a long way from the thought that theories of the atonement might be three or four in number. That always had been a simplification, even an oversimplification. But the question raised by Aulén about the impossibility of a theory returns even more insistently. Are we obliged, in recognising the rich plurality of ideas associated with atonement, absolutely to abandon all hope of an explanation? Should, as Aulén demanded, all theories or demands for a theory be rejected as rationalistic?

WHAT IS A 'THEORY' OF ATONEMENT?

In the Oxford English Dictionary a theory is defined as a 'scheme or system of ideas or statements held as an explanation or account of a group of facts or phenomena'. To this I would merely add that the intensity of demand for a theory varies in accordance with the surprising character of the facts or phenomenon. The appearance of ghosts, UFOs or extra-terrestrial beings strongly suggests the need for a theory, even one which tries to give an account of why the individuals experiencing them believe they perceive what they claim to perceive; a theory about a subject's state of mind is still a theory. In ordinary Christian experience, one may well want a theory to account for unusual occurrences like contemporary miracles or speaking in tongues. At the same time there is not much demand for a theory of hymn-singing, odd though that activity is in some ways. A theory is an explanation that attempts to reduce surprise.

In Christian theology the statements which cause the surprise are credal, and ultimately biblical. 'For us and for our salvation he came down from heaven'; 'he was crucified, dead and buried for us'. One of the earliest 'theories' of atonement was contained in Anselm's book *Cur Deus Homo*, translated either 'Why did God become man?' or 'Why God became man'.[11] In other words it offered an explanatory answer to a question about a very surprising fact (or alleged fact). The point of the book, which develops its arguments quite apart from the interpretation of texts of the New Testament, is to discover the *ratio*, the principle of coherence, within the *revelatio*, God's own self-disclosure.

Would this really be an example of rationalism, as Aulén suggested? If so, what do we have to say about the enterprise of theology itself? What connections, if any, are there between living the Christian life, and providing ourselves with theories or explanations to answer the questions which may be raised about some surprising Christian affirmations?

The passage already cited from the letter to Hebrews takes us a certain way. The author is plainly irritated with those who have proved slow to learn, who are infants in the faith, stuck on the rudiments of Christianity. The author wants them to advance to maturity and warns vividly against the danger of relapsing. There is before them a 'promised inheritance', which he wants to expound, and he has to do so, he says, by making clear why it is that Jesus has given us an absolutely safe anchor for our lives. This is the context in which he asserts that we have, in Jesus, a high priest in the eternal order of Melchizedek, who has entered the sanctuary on our behalf as a forerunner (Heb. 10:19–20).

But who on earth is Melchizedek, and what has he to do with Jesus?[12] All that now follows is plainly theory, or explanation designed to remove the surprise caused by the original statement. Nor is the statement in any way abstract or remote from Christian life. We grasp the hope that is set before us precisely because we understand what Christ has done. He has offered himself as the final and complete sacrifice for sin; he has opened up for us a 'living way' through the curtain, the way of his own flesh; and it is because this high priest has been set over God's household that we have the rights of approach to God in sincerity of heart and full assurance of faith. Immediately there follow words in which we note the speedy application of doctrine to practice.

11

> Let us be firm and unswerving in the profession of our
> faith, for the giver of the promise is to be trusted. We ought
> to see how each of us may best arouse others to love and
> active goodness. We should not stay away from our meetings
> as some do. (Heb. 10:23–5)

The argument comes within a whisker of descending into
banality, so close is the association of high doctrine and
practical church life.

This example from Hebrews forces us to confront the
questions already mentioned about the author's presuppo-
sitions concerning the Old Testament. But if these matters
are raised, all one can say is that *further* effort at explanation is called for. If a theory or explanation related to
Melchizedek will not do, then we shall need a better one.
Explanations are not in themselves rationalistic; and on
the evidence of Hebrews they lend themselves to highly
practical applications and conclusions. For this reason I
find Aulén's rejection of theory unconvincing. The fact
that *some* theories seem remote, abstract or even morally
objectionable, does not mean that all theories are necessarily so. Theories arise because there are questions to be
asked. The fact that theories themselves lead to further
puzzles, or are incomplete, is not an adequate ground for
denying that they have explanatory value. We shall see the
situation more clearly if we attend for a moment to
the precise context in which the questions arise. This is the
context of story, of narrative, on which I propose to
concentrate at this point.

NARRATIVES OF ATONEMENT

There is a 'story of salvation'. This story, like all narratives,
is a combination of character and event in interaction.[13]
At its heart lies the 'sacred history' of Jesus, as told in the

gospels. This is no ordinary story, because all that happens is preceded by the rubric, 'Who for us and for our salvation, came down from heaven'. The simplest way of seeing the story is to understand the creed as the bare bones of a story, though not in any literary sense a narrative. It is capable of being understood, or at least learnt, by relatively young people. It is simple and precise – and, as John Henry Newman once wrote, 'to be simple and precise in fundamentals is a socially charitable arrangement, so that all classes might profess the same faith in the same terms, the totality be easily memorable, and minds be saved from perplexity'.[14] Behind the credal narrative lies the fuller text of the gospel, and so the person reciting it may use the lines as a series of pegs on which to hang conscious or unconscious recollections and reflections. The familiar words, 'Who on the same night that he was betrayed', recall the fact that Jesus was betrayed by one of his close friends; the poignancy of the worshipper having already made confession of his or her sin is implicitly stressed. Jesus is remembered as having known about his betrayal, and yet not having acted to frustrate it. The ambivalence of complicity in the world's evil is suggested, at the same time as Jesus' steadfastness in his vocation. In this way credal recitation becomes the carrier of richer layers of meaning and emotion, a range of implication (to cite Newman again) 'incomprehensible in its depth and indefinite in its extent'.[15]

The closer analysis of the 'grammar of narrative', the implicit rules which enable us to construe a series of sentences as a narrative of some kind, contain four elements in sequence:

- the setting
- the theme
- the plot or plots

• the resolution.

In the case of the story of Red Riding Hood, the opening words ('Once upon a time, there was a little girl called Red Riding Hood, whose granny lived in a cottage in a forest') supplies the *setting*; the *theme* is the struggle with the wolf; the *plot* concerns the journey into the forest; and the *resolution* is the slaying of the wolf.

In Christian narrative, God's world is the *setting*; the *theme* is the rescue of the fallen world and of humankind from destruction; the *plots* are the biblical narratives, from creation and election, to incarnation, crucifixion, resurrection and ascension; the *resolution* is the last judgement, heaven and hell, and the new creation. This, as I have suggested, is the bare outline of the story. There are a variety of ways of telling it, just as there are four gospels. We shall shortly examine one vivid and influential way in which this story has been told – by Milton in *Paradise Lost*. But we need now to find some way of focusing upon the 'story of the cross' as the story whose theme is the atoning for human sin.

On the face of it, the narratives from the gospels simply tell us that Jesus of Nazareth was betrayed by one of his disciples to the Jewish authorities, who found a way of getting the Roman governor, Pontius Pilate, to put him to death.[16] But then God raised Jesus to life, and for a short time he appeared to his disciples before being taken up into heaven. On closer inspection, the gospel narratives say much more than this. For example, they make clear that details of the story exactly correspond to prophecies in the Old Testament, so that what happens can be seen by the reader to be within the will and counsel of God. Or again, on the night of his betrayal, Jesus takes a solemn meal with his disciples, in the course of which he offers an interpretation of his own death. The narratives, in other

14

words, are already set within a specific plot, which is engaged in working out the theme of human redemption. The plots interpret the theme and advance it towards the resolution. The plots involve characters and events in inter-action, and the narrative does not allow the reader to forget that God is the main agent in the whole narrative. Although the events may concern Judas Iscariot, or Simon Peter, or Pontius Pilate, or Caiaphas, the intentions of God as an agent in the narrative are never far below the surface.

At the same time, so far from being self-explanatory the narrative of the crucifixion elicits enormous surprise, and cries out for an explanation. Here is Jesus, the Son of God, seeking not to do his own will but the will of one he calls his heavenly Father, accepting – indeed embracing – an unjust deed as his own vocation and destiny. Why? The event demands explanation. Why should God ask this of Jesus, named his beloved Son? Why should this life, death and resurrection have such power? Not one, but a variety of explanatory hints is given. Particularly helpful in this regard is Joachim Jeremias' suggestion that the New Testa-ment contains what he calls 'clusters of idea-complexes' to explain the surprising fact of the crucifixion as God's will. He distinguishes four such idea-complexes:[17]

1   the idea of obedience, contrasting Adam's dis-obedience with the obedience of the second Adam;
2   the slavery idea, relating to redemption and setting free;
3   the judgement idea, relating to condemnation and acquittal;
4   the cultic idea, relating to sacrifice (Passover lamb, the blood of Jesus, the sinless offering, a substitute goat).

Atonement theology, properly so called, Jeremias argues, develops after the New Testament period out of these hints and suggestions, most of which are undeveloped in their New Testament contexts.

I should like to elaborate on Jeremias' suggestion by showing how the themes or idea-complexes are, in fact, suppressed or implicit narratives. The letter to the Romans, for example, never tells the story of our redemption in so many words, but if you work hard at some of the classic passages you can see the elements of the narrative at various points. The most obvious example is the theme of obedience, which quite explicitly invites the reader to recall the narrative of Adam and to contrast it with the narrative of Jesus. By itself the theme does not completely explain why 'one man's obedience makes many people righteous' (Rom. 5:19). Why should it? But the narrative of Jesus' life is necessary if the proposal is to have any merit at all, and in rehearsing it we are invited to see in it the record of Jesus' *perfect* obedience; in other words, it embodies a reversal of every other human narrative or life-story. And the sinlessness of Jesus' life is a vital aspect of more than one way of explaining the power of the life, death and resurrection of Jesus.

Slavery, too, is a fairly specific and concrete theme in the narrative. Human beings are enslaved to Satan. Jesus pays the price of manumission, with the result that humankind is set free. Redemption is the key word in a narrative which represents Jesus as both the liberator and the price of liberation. Slavery is, in effect, a metaphor for the consequence of sin, and the story is an imaginary narrative reconstructing the motive behind God's liberating action. Because we are enslaved (to sin), God's action in Jesus is the expression of his will for our redemption, Jesus himself being the agent of our liberation and his own life-giving the extreme cost of our manumission.

The theme of judgement lends itself to the same kind of treatment. By our wrongdoing we incur guilt and deserve punishment. But instead of condemning us, God our judge acquits us and counts us free of guilt, having accepted the death of Christ as the equivalent penalty for our transgressions. In this way, too, judgement and acquittal stand as a metaphor for what is involved in sin and its forgiveness, accomplished at-one-ment or the reconciliation to each other of estranged parties by the gracious action of one of them.

Finally, the cultic cluster of ideas, though on the face of it referring simply to a symbolic event (that of sacrifice or ritual scapegoating), also needs to be set in a narrative context if it is to be understood. What makes the life of Jesus a holy sacrifice is the quality and course of his life's work, and the intention to which he gives expression. Jesus' sacrifice for sin is a self-offering. We need to know this, if we are to speak of Jesus as the Lamb of God. He is not simply an innocent and uncomprehending victim. He understands and accepts what is happening, and gives it his own specific meaning. Just as the Passover sacrifice and meal occurs within the specific narrative of the Exodus, so the death of Christ as sacrifice needs to be recollected in the whole context triggered by the words, 'Who, in the same night that he was betrayed'.

From this it becomes clear that although there is a story of salvation – in the credal sense of a brief summary of Jesus' actions for us and for our salvation – there is a plurality of narratives for atonement. These arise out of, and are implied by, the idea-complexes which we have examined. It is characteristic of the New Testament – and of much theological communication – to allude to, rather than to spell out, the implied narrative. For this reason it often looks as though the right way to speak of atonement theology is in a series of metaphors – the metaphor of judgement, the metaphor of sacrifice, and so forth.[18] Nor is this wrong, provided metaphor is not treated as 'mere metaphor', to be disposed of in the interests of real or literal explanation. But in many cases the currency of the metaphor depends upon its being sustained by a plausible narrative. This is the advantage of the thought that the New Testament sponsors a series of idea-complexes. Many of these are actually metaphors in the contexts in which they are used, but are linked in the imagery they invoke to a range of other similar ideas. All of them, taken as a complex unity, depend upon a narrative: they are ways of reading the story of Jesus, the stories of the gospels, the story of our redemption.

In one case of supposed metaphor, the Christian tradition has, so to speak, deliberately reversed the flow of reference (this will be examined more closely in chapter 5). This concerns sacrifice. There were, of course, literal sacrifices being performed in the Temple at the time of Jesus' life and death. But Christian theology quickly came to claim that Christ's death was the one true sacrifice; and that other sacrifices were at best foreshadowings of that sacrifice. There are several important theological words which were originally metaphorical, and in a sense remain so, but whose first meaning is only a faint analogue of the truth of their full significance.[19] Sacrifice is one such word. Neither Jewish nor pagan sacrifice provide theology with its fundamental meaning. It will be argued that the narrative of Christ's sacrifice is normative for understanding what real sacrifice is. There are modern analogues, as there were ancient ones, for this basic meaning. The fact that cultic sacrifices of crops or animals are no longer widely made is largely irrelevant to the present-day currency of the concept. We have our own lethal ways of deploying the term sacrifice in relation to warfare and terrorism. To save it from abuse, this so-called metaphor must be rooted in the unique story of Jesus' way to his death, in his intentions and actions and their astonishing sequences.

QUESTIONS ABOUT GOD AND JESUS

The narratives give rise to further questions, primarily because the intentions and will of God (as an agent in the narrative) are still obscure and surprising. The issue obviously arises as to whether or not we can give any more elaborated explanations which might reduce the level of surprise. For example, a classic question in the early history of atonement theology was whether, because of the fall and human sinfulness, the Devil had acquired rights over humanity in such a way that human redemption could only be achieved if God paid *to the Devil* what was owing to him. Anselm appears to accept criticism of this way of construing the narrative, as giving too much independent power over against God.

Another such question is whether the death of Jesus is the equivalent penalty for human sin, without which the acquittal of guilty human beings is impossible; and if that is so, whether God himself is guilty of vengefulness in requiring suffering rather than offering forgiveness. The implications of this objection are that God's attitude and action towards sin seems to conflict with the attitude and actions recommended of a Christian. How can this be? On the other hand, if God were not to treat sin as sin, how could God be regarded as just and holy? God's love and God's justice seem to require contrasting, if not contradictory, policies. Can they be reconciled in a single narrative? Can we construct the narrative of God's intentions and actions towards humankind in such a way that they do not present an unattractive, contradictory or impossible-to-believe principle agent?

A long-overdue consideration must be introduced here – namely the unsatisfactoriness of reducing the being and reality of God to that of an agent in a narrative. This unsatisfactoriness arises from two familiar doctrines: those of the Trinity and of God's transcendence. In the case of the Trinity, it is bound to lead to difficulty if God the Father and Jesus the Son are simply represented as separate characters in the story. In the Interlude attached to this chapter we shall trace the consequences of this in Milton's epic *Paradise Lost* Book III, which makes a heroic attempt to interpret the motives of God and the consequences of Christ's death in a single story-line. According to this narrative, the Father outlines to the Son the catastrophic situation of humanity; the Son asks how is it possible that the Father's will could be finally frustrated; the Father replies that, without a 'rigid satisfaction, death for death', humanity is doomed; and he asks for a redeemer. Eventually the Son volunteers to let God's anger fall on him. The Father accepts the offer, and promises to impute merit to all who put their trust in the Son. In other words, Father and Son negotiate the terms of atonement in a kind of heavenly council chamber, after which the Son sets out to fulfil his part of the bargain. The doctrine of the Trinity is reduced to the fact that Father and Son are, eventually, in agreement with each other, and both act out of motives of love and grace. This is not a satisfactory representation of classic Trinitarianism, and the Milton of *Paradise Lost* was, indeed, an Arian, who believed the Son to be subordinate in dignity.

Nor does this way of telling the story adequately represent the sense in which neither God the Father, nor the Son, nor the Spirit, are characters in a narrative, in the strict sense in which human beings are characters in a narrative. Anthropomorphism is, precisely, the ascription of human form and attributes to the deity; and it offends against the doctrine of the transcendent otherness of God, his incomprehensibility. We may claim to know God, or, more precisely, to know his self-revelation. We may not claim to understand or comprehend God, who is beyond our comprehension. The trouble with the narrative mode is that it offers no alternative but to represent God by analogy with a human agent in a story. But we are bound to add, if we are true to Christian theology, that the motives, intentions and will of *God* are not comprehended in the motives, intentions and will attributed to the God of whom we speak in our narratives.

The two criticisms of our narratives, the Trinitarian and the transcendent, combine in the observation that it will not do simply to represent Father and Son as engaged in a negotiation over the impasse of grace and punishment, love and justice. It is more satisfactory to separate out two somewhat different types of story, one in which the leading agent is God the Father, who out of love for the world and humanity, provides and puts forward nothing less than his very own substance (his only Son) as the final remedy for sin. This is the implication of the narrative in Mark 12, which concerns the problem of the landowner and his rebellious tenants. The question is entirely seen from the standpoint of the landowner and his rights to the harvest of his fields. The interest, motives and intentions of the son, his heir, whom he eventually sends, are not part of the narrative in any sense. The owner's last resort is to send his son, who is also killed. The landowner is furious and prepares for vengeance. (We should compare the poet, George Herbert's, rendering of this narrative in *Redemption*, where the 'rich landowner' is, in fact, the son himself, thus giving a more Trinitarian emphasis to the narrative.)[20] Similarly, classic statements such as 'God so loved the world that he gave his only Son' (John 3:16), focus upon the divine love and gift in making provision for human salvation.

But there is another group of narratives which focuses upon Jesus, the Son of God, who gives or offers himself out of love for humanity, and does so freely and without

21

compulsion. This is the natural implication of the narrative of the Synoptic Gospels, especially of the story of Gethsemane, or in the Gospel of John, of the high priestly prayer (chapter 17). Here, the obvious motivation is Jesus' loving response of obedience to the Father's will, as the prototype of human response to God's love. The central agency is emphatically human, so the representation of response to God presents no Trinitarian problem (though it was in due course to cause difficulties for understanding the relationship of Christ's divine and human natures).

The point of separating the narratives is to make intelligible certain key features of the Christian understanding of atonement. In the first story, what emerges is God's grace in not allowing humankind simply to reap the full consequence of sin. In a situation in which we were helpless to save ourselves, God takes the initiative out of love for his creation; and the cost to God of that initiative is the giving of his own self and substance. The divine creator of world accepts the price of the freedom of creaturehood, and does so in the being of his only Son. In the second story what is emphasised is Jesus' own self-offering. He loves his own who are in the world 'to the end' (John 13:1). There is no external compulsion; he is not an impersonal means or instrument. He freely subordinates his own will to the will of his heavenly Father. The difference between the drift of the two stories can be put in this way: whereas it is in the interest of the first story to link the Father and the Son, it is in the interest of the second to separate them.

Our instinct is to empathise with the second. Human beings are perfectly familiar with situations where we acquiesce, more or less willingly, with what we know to be someone else's will or desire for us. A moment's thought, however, shows us the difference. The relation of Father and Son is not of two coinciding but independent rational wills. We buy intelligibility at the cost of making the Father's act of 'sending' his Son a morally disgraceful act. Why should the Father will the death of the Son? Should the Father not have suffered the consequences himself? We have no human analogies strong enough for the Trinitarian reply, that the Father did indeed participate in the suffering of his Son.

The history of theological argument in the first six centuries shows how intensely these very issues were debated. 'No Entry' signs were erected over certain superficially attractive solutions – for example, the simple idea that the Father suffered what the Son suffered ('patripassianism'), or that there was only one will in Christ ('monothelitism'). The orthodox formulations of Trinitarianism were, in effect, no solution of any kind. They were rather indications of the complexity and intensity of the problem – a kind of exclamation mark. But both of the narratives which underlay this more abstract theological work were necessary, in that they motivated the endeavour. It is no surprise to have to admit to their inadequacies.

I have taken a rather strong view that there is a story of our salvation, and that it can be easily communicated in outline even if it exists in a plurality of narrative versions. But it has recently become axiomatic in philosophy that the 'great stories' have failed and must be completely given up.[21] I am not convinced. What does this so-called failure mean? If it means that not all people live in, or are persuaded by, one overarching narrative, that is no surprise. The Church's great story was originally the conviction of a tiny minority in the context of a riotous diversity of alternatives. If there is criticism of the fact that such a story is a concentration of power, again this is hardly astonishing. The gospel is 'the power of God for salvation', according to Paul. Only if all power were assumed to be domination, and thus illegitimate or immoral, could such criticism be taken as a final objection. The Church may well have to claim, against the drift of what is termed 'post-modernism', that it *is* offering a great story, that the story claims to be true, that it originates in God's own actions and has the power to transform individuals and societies.

But one concession can easily be made – indeed, it has already been acknowledged. Inside the multiple versions of the story there is ample space for improvisation and imaginative freedom. It seems that the 'great story' exists in our head in snatches, so to speak. We have a sense of its having the shape of a story, with a setting, theme, plot(s) and resolution – but the plot or plots can be told in episodes, and the episodes lend themselves to different versions. There is enough coherence to provide a unity, but not so much definitive detail as to stifle the capacity for improvisation on the theme.

In this connection a recent writer has described the churches' task as 'providing the pieces, materials and resources out of which a new world can be imagined', and the Scriptures as a 'compost pile' providing the enrichment for new life.[22] But there is one respect in which these resources must cohere, that is in respect of God's faithfulness to his covenant. It is crucial to Christian life and faith that we can say, with confidence, that God has a will of love towards the world and humankind. There is no way in which we can be assured of this except by a narrative which lays out God's character as shown in his deeds and intentions. Just as in a good marriage all kinds of exigencies can be accommodated where there is full confidence in a partner's fidelity and goodwill, so human life is radically changed by the knowledge that nothing whatever can separate us from the love of God which is in Jesus Christ (Rom. 8:39); 'in Jesus Christ' meaning what Jesus shows of his being known to us through the stories of the gospels. It is greatly to Milton's credit that this consistent goodness of will emerges so clearly in his epic retelling of the story of salvation, to which we now turn.

ooooooooooo

Justifying the ways of God in Milton's *Paradise Lost*

Is it possible to tell the 'story of the atonement' as a single continuous narrative, which is at the same time credible? To be sure, the word 'credible' begs a number of questions. No account of the atonement has ever been immediately persuasive to everyone who heard or read it. Instead of 'credible' we may settle for a lesser aspiration, that of being free of immediate moral objection. So, can the story be told in such a way that the motives and actions of the leading characters are consistent and intelligible, and the result involves no obvious form of moral contradiction? While recognising that there are those who argue that no form of Christian atonement theology could be, or is, consistent with the way the world is, it is worth addressing this question, critically, as a matter of internal consistency for Christian theology itself.

Milton's *Paradise Lost*, composed in the turbulent years of mid seventeenth-century England, published in 1667 after the Restoration and revised in 1674, offers us a magnificent example of the full sweep of an atonement narrative.

> Of Man's first disobedience, and the fruit
> Of that forbidden tree, whose mortal taste
> Brought death into the world, and all our woe,

> With loss of Eden, till one greater man
> Restore us, and regain that blissful seat,
> Sing, Heavenly Muse.
>
> (I, 1–6)[1]

Milton realises that he is not simply a narrator, but that his theme constitutes an argument or apology for the truth of the faith. So he asks for the assistance of the Holy Spirit.

> And chiefly thou, O Spirit, that dost prefer
> Before all temples the upright heart and pure,
> Instruct me, for thou know'st . . .
> . . . What in me is dark
> Illumine, what is low raise and support;
> That the highth of this great argument
> I may assert eternal providence,
> And justify the ways of God to men.
>
> (I, 17–26)

Paradise Lost opens with an account of Satan and his angels in hell, plotting in rage and hatred some revenge on God for their defeat and banishment from heaven. Having lost the first battle in open combat, they decide to work by fraud or guile.

Book II gives an account of how, in another world, humankind is about to be created – creatures whose vulnerability presents a suitable target for satanic spite. But comments Milton, 'their spite still serves/His [God's] glory to augment' (II, 385–6). If glory is to shine forth, the shaping of the epic has to give a plausible account of the reason for the Fall of Adam and Eve. Then, because it is Satan who is blamed for that fall, there has also to be a plausible account of why Satan is in existence and has the limited power he still possesses. Milton makes clear that the capacities of Satan and his angels remain, such as they are, by:

27

the will
And high permission of all-ruling heaven.

(I, 212)

So when Satan sets off from his own domain for the world,
again Milton insists that the ruinous consequences for
humanity are still according to 'the will of heaven' (II,
1025).

The twofold justification for this state of affairs lies in
the positive value of human freedom, and the glory of the
redemption. Book III, upon which we shall focus, gives a
vivid account of both of these vital features of the narrative.
It presents God the Almighty Father, seated in majesty in
the heavens, and beside him his Son, 'the radiant image
of his glory' (III, 63). Together they consider the implications of Satan's approach to the world. The Father
explicitly foresees Adam's weakness and fall, and makes
plain that he could have withstood temptation. Moreover,
if Adam had not been free to fall, neither would he have
been free to respond in 'true allegiance, constant faith or
love' (III, 104). To have served God out of necessity would
not have expressed the personal relationship for which
humankind was created. God foreknows the Fall, but does
not foreordain it; so God cannot be blamed for it. Milton
distinguishes between the primordial fall of the angels and
that of Adam. The fall of Satan and the angels was by their
own suggestion, 'self-tempted, self-depraved' (III, 130); for
them, therefore, there is no redemption. But humanity
fell by deception of Satan:

Man therefore shall find grace,
The other none: in mercy and justice both,
Through heaven and earth, so shall my glory excel,
But mercy first and last shall brightest shine.

(III, 131–4)

28

This argument is designed to meet the charge that an omnipotent God has to accept responsibility for the existence of evil in the world; but that acceptance contradicts the concept of 'omnipotence', and therefore the Christian account of the world falls by reason of internal self-contradiction. Milton's reply is still deployed in modern theology, and is known as 'the free-will defence'.[2] Equally modern is the plain limit his account gives to divine omnipotence. Though he refers (or gets Satan to refer) to God as 'the omnipotent' (I, 49), he also significantly uses the term 'almighty'. Modern theology has refined the distinction between 'omnipotence' and 'almightiness'.[3] Milton's account explicitly and repeatedly makes clear that God's 'almighty power' still permits the countervailing power of Satan (and, by implication of human freedom, also of humanity) its own proper sphere of exercise. Imaginary epic though this may be, its nuances are of no small continuing importance in modern theology.

We can be more precise than this. The question is, what conceivable motives or intention can God have had in bringing the world we experience into existence? The question is a proper one to address to Christian theology because God is, according to the Christian account, personal and good. To speak of God as an impersonal Life-Force or Energy would fundamentally contradict Trinitarian theology and the emphasis on God's love in the world's creation and redemption. Milton's epic or narrative permits, indeed requires, him to attribute to God a worthy and credible motive in bringing humankind into existence. God is presented as an agent in the narrative, almighty but discernibly personal. God's motives cannot be casual, unreflective or base: that would contradict the attribution of wisdom and goodness to God. Yet such attributes are necessarily pressed by the facts of suffering and evil. Could there not have been a less costly way of providing the good of human freedom? To answer that perennial question lies at the heart of Milton's attempt to 'justify the ways of God to men', and to provide a theodicy credible to his contemporaries.[4]

Book III advances the argument substantially by means of a dialogue in heaven between the Father and the Son. In response to God's account of the culpability of humanity in the (future and foreseen) fall, the Son speaks in praise of the Father's grace:

> O Father, gracious was that word which closed
> Thy sovereign sentence, that man should find grace.
> For which both heaven and earth shall high extol
> Thy praises, with the innumerable sound
> Of hymns and sacred songs, wherewith thy throne
> Encompassed shall resound thee ever blest.
>
> (III, 144–9)

God's motive and intention is thus identified as gracious, and the outcome is the outpouring of hymns of praise and the augmenting of God's glory. Given that human beings must be free to respond in obedience or disobedience to God's call, the outcome of the Fall jeopardises the whole purpose of creation. Human beings were created for God's glory, not for corruption in hell:

> So should thy goodness and thy greatness both
> Be questioned and blasphemed without defence.
>
> (III, 165–6)

The dilemma's solution with which Milton feels most comfortable, and on which he wants to comment, was called Arminianism in the seventeenth century, after a Dutch Reformed pastor named Jacobus Arminius (1560–1609). This was a reorientation of Reformed (that is, Calvinist) theology in order to make it more acceptable to common-sense notions of freedom and justice. It specifically involved the claim, denied by Calvin, that the efficacy of Christ's sacrifice extended to all human beings, not just the elect. Each individual is granted the opportunity of sufficient grace. Salvation is still not within a person's unaided power: it depends wholly on grace. But, as Milton himself puts it, in words attributed to the Father:

> I will clear their senses dark,
> What may suffice, and soften stony hearts
> To pray, repent, and bring obedience due . . .
> And I will place within them as a guide
> My umpire conscience, whom if they will hear,
> Light after light well used they shall attain,
> And to the end persisting, safe arrive.
>
> (III, 188–90, 194–7)

No one is excluded from this possibility. But for such grace to be effective, more is needed. Adam's treasonable transgression against heaven must have a specific remedy; otherwise justice would demand his death, and the death of the whole human race.

What then is to be done? The situation is identified by the Father in the form of the starkest alternative:

> Die he or justice must; unless for him
> Some other able, and as willing, pay
> The rigid satisfaction, death for death.
> Say, heavenly powers, where shall we find such love?
>
> (III, 210–13)

Here comes into view the particular way in which Milton, following a vast Christian tradition, conceives of the atonement. The consequence of Adam's disobedience is death as a punishment. If Adam were not to be punished for his sin by death, then justice would not be done, and God's own being would be contradicted. The only foreseeable alternative is a 'rigid satisfaction', the payment by someone

31

of an absolutely equivalent penalty. Anselm, six centuries earlier, had formulated the matter conceptually in a similar though not identical way. Either humanity must be punished with death, or a satisfaction for the dishonour done to God must be offered. Sin cannot be merely overlooked as though it were not sin.[5] Milton makes the dilemma personal, by having God the Father ask where such love could be found to make so remarkable a satisfaction.

The drama is immediately heightened when it is made clear that none of the heavenly choir is willing to step forward as the intercessor for humanity, still less to pay the ransom price. In the poignant silence the Son now speaks:

> Father, thy word is past, man shall find grace;
> And shall Grace not find means, that finds her way,
> The speediest of thy winged messengers,
> To visit all thy creatures, and to all
> Comes unprevented, unimplored, unsought?
>
> (III, 227–31)

The motive assigned by Milton for the atonement is God's grace. The Son precisely quotes the Father's words, 'Man shall find grace', and immediately offers himself as the satisfaction:

> Behold me then, me for him, life for life,
> I offer, on me let thine anger fall;
> Account me man; I for his sake will leave
> Thy bosom, and this glory next to thee
> Freely put off, and for him lastly die
> Well pleased; on me let Death wreak all his rage.
>
> (III, 236–41)

In these words, Milton embraces what is known as the theory of penal satisfaction – that is, the satisfaction which is offered is a death endured as God's wrathful punishment due to human sin. In this way the requirement of God's justice is thought to be preserved, and Christ is both the satisfaction and the punished victim. What Anselm presents as an alternative – either punishment or satisfaction – is by Milton, following some major Reformation thinkers, fused. The punishment of Christ, though innocent, *is* the satisfaction.

None the less we note Milton's pains to present Christ as freely offering his own death, and doing so out of love. It is not the case, at least not in the narrative, that the Father demands the offering of the death of his Son. But Milton knows of the theme of filial obedience from Romans 5 ('through the obedience of one man many will be made righteous', v. 19). Does not the Son, therefore, obey the Father in offering his life? If so, does not the Father command that offering? Milton wants to have it both ways:

> His words here ended, but his meek aspect
> Silent yet spake, and breathed immortal love
> To mortal men, above which only shone,
> Filial obedience: as a sacrifice
> Glad to be offered, he attends the will
> Of his great Father.
>
> (III, 266–71)

Everything is embraced within God's will. But, as we have already seen, that will can be permissive rather than predestinating. The will of the Son freely consents to God's will, but is not coerced by it.

The narrative proceeds with the Father accepting the self-offering of the Son, and determining that the Son shall be joined to human nature, in the birth from the Virgin. Milton's account of the reversal of Adam's disobedience, told in Romans 5, is as follows:

> His crime makes guilty all his sons, thy merit
> Imputed shall absolve them who renounce
> Their own both righteous and unrighteous deeds,
> And live in thee transplanted, and from thee
> Receive new life.
>
> (III, 290–4)

Adam's crime is outweighed by Christ's merit, which merit is imputed (a common Reformation term) to those who abandon not merely their vices, but also confidence in their own virtues. Such people have been 'transplanted', a metaphor recalling 'abiding in the true vine' of the Fourth Gospel (John 15).

This is the plan, foreseen as a way of frustrating Satan's attempt to take revenge upon God by deceiving humanity, and its announcement in the heavens elicits another paean of praise. The self-offering of the Son is presented as utterly admirable in its generous meeting of the impasse of 'the strife of mercy and justice' (III, 406–7) in God. And the outcome increases the glory of God, the narrative of God's dealings with creation as a whole has a positive character. God's glory is augmented; his way is justified. That at least is the overt purpose of Milton's epic.

But the narrative gives rise to questions. Some of the questions bear upon matters which Milton simply assumes from tradition, and never examines. It is true, for example, that the guilt of human sin requires death as its punishment? Is it morally tolerable, for example, to imply that the damnation and punishment of unbaptised infants is required as due punishment for the guilt of their ancestor Adam? And is it the case that justice requires a 'rigid satisfaction'? Do you have to break the leg of someone who breaks your leg? Does not justice also accept *equivalent* penalties, for example monetary fines for physical wrongs? Some of these puzzles had been examined by earlier theologians. Anselm's answer to why God became man was that it enabled a *greater* offering (both an equivalent, and infinitely more) to be made by humanity in Christ's human person. Christ's death, therefore, was the enduring not of a just punishment, but of a monstrous injustice, as a consequence of which the Devil forfeited his usurped tyranny over humankind. Milton, however, stands in a tradition strongly influenced by the reformers for whom the finality of a full substitution, bringing the Father's wrath against sin to an end, had proved powerfully attractive.

That tradition did apparently involve, however, a distinction between the Father who punishes and the Son who placates. It was not a satisfactory narrative: John Donne (1571–1631) told his congregation, 'Never consider the judgement of God for sin alone, but in the company of the mercies of Christ'.[6] A modern commentator urges us to see the dialogue in *Paradise Lost* between Father and Son as taking place with the Unity of the Godhead.[7] But it is not possible to forget that Milton was an Arian, for whom the Son was a subordinate within the Godhead. The story of the dialogue in heaven does not work otherwise, and he accepts its logic.

For all its faults as theology, Milton's epic is exceptionally enlightening. As we have already seen, some of its clarifications of the divine intentions are still current, because, I suggest, the questions it addresses are perennial. It is still necessary to form some conception of God's foreknowledge of the fallen human condition, even without the myth of a fall from primal innocence. It is also necessary to have some theological reflection on Jesus' intentions regarding his consent to his own death. Jesus' words in St Matthew's gospel, 'Not my will but yours' (Matt. 26:39), spoken in Gethsemane and thus already set within a narrative, need the broader context which the epic form gives them. It is precisely the narrative which conveys the complexity of what requires theological analysis. We may judge that Milton's single, continuous narrative of the atonement fails the test of credibility at certain significant points; nevertheless the effort which it represents is irreplaceable, and the questions to which it gives rise are unavoidable.

2

oooooooooo

Justification by faith

We begin, again, with forgiveness. But on this occasion
we take a more problematic aspect of this desired
and desirable feature of life. How, if I am the offender,
can I be really sure that I have been forgiven? There is,
after all, such a thing as partial forgiveness in ordinary
human experience. The one I have injured may *say* that
the wrong has been forgiven, but how do I know? Has it
been forgiven in such a way that I do not have, for the
next weeks, months or even years, to walk round that
person as though upon eggshells? Can I be sure that
hidden resentments may not come bursting out at some
subsequent occasion? Is it perhaps the case that the un-
acknowledged motive for forgiveness may be a desire to
trap me in a net of unending obligation? Or could it not
even be a deliberate calculation to defer revenge? None
of this can apparently be known for certain.

The problem was vividly illustrated when, on the fiftieth
anniversary of the ending of the second world war, Allied
soldiers who served in Japanese prisoner-of-war camps were
offered by the prime minister of Japan an apology for
the inhumanity of their treatment. But was the apology
enough? What about financial compensation for their
injuries, beyond the meagre terms agreed at the subsequent peace conference? Was this politician's apology
even sincere? Could any apology be adequate for the injustice of the loss by torture or starvation of even one life?

37

The public heard a bewildering variety of views from the veterans: for some, no apology could ever provoke forgiveness; some wanted public humiliations; some wanted more compensation; some said they forgave. The issue apparently is, can there be such a thing as unconditional forgiveness? That is precisely the question with which the theological doctrine of justification by faith – or rather justification by grace to be received by faith – deals.

St Paul is explicit enough: 'Therefore, now that we have been justified through faith, we are at peace with God through our Lord Jesus Christ, who has given us access to that grace in which we now live' (Rom. 5:1–2). Peace with God is at-one-ment; a peace without caveats or reservations, a generous, thorough, beautiful and life-creating new start. A book on atonement is bound to deal substantially with justification, and the first task is to grasp the correct context for the subject – that is, sin and its forgiveness, which will occupy us in the first instance. But we shall also need to take account of two problems of some difficulty, the first about the relationship between Jesus' teaching and that of St Paul, and the second concerning the serious rifts about justification which occurred in the sixteenth-century Protestant Reformation.

JUSTIFICATION AND SIN

Justification is unintelligible as a theological term unless we take seriously the *reality of sin*. There is no difficulty in showing this connection from the relevant texts of the New Testament, almost all of which set the term specifically and expressly in that context. The opening chapter of Romans is a good example. Paul begins by sending his greetings, and by saying how he longs to visit the congregation, expressing his 'eagerness to declare the gospel to you in Rome as well' (v.16). Of this gospel he is not ashamed. It is the power of God to all who have faith. Then follow the clarifying words: 'In it [that is, the gospel] the righteousness [*dikaiosyne*] of God is seen at work, beginning in faith and ending in faith; as scripture says, "Whoever is justified through faith shall gain life"' (Rom. 1:17).

The scripture quotation is from Habakkuk 2:4; but this, however, immediately suggests to Paul the necessity of showing that God's justifying activity is set against the background of sin and wrongdoing. In the text of Habakkuk, the words 'the righteous will live by being faithful' (REB translation of the Hebrew – Paul is, apparently, quoting a Greek version of the text from memory) are both preceded and followed by contrasting statements about the reckless, the conceited, the treacherous and the arrogant. Just as those constitute the backcloth, so to speak, to the faithful righteous in Habakkuk's time, so for Paul the fact of human wickedness among both Gentiles and Jews is the context of God's justifying activity.

Indeed, the next sections of Romans are devoted to showing how 'divine retribution' or wrath is to be seen at work, falling on all Gentiles who in their impiety and wickedness suppress the truth, and also on all Jews who, however scrupulous, none the less break God's law and thus incur guilt. Summarising this bleak analysis are the well-known words, 'All alike have sinned, and are deprived of God's glory' (Rom. 3:23). This is the only conceivable context for the affirmation which follows: 'and all alike are justified by God's free grace alone, through his act of liberation in the person of Christ Jesus' (Rom. 3:24). The passage then naturally goes on to discuss the reality of the divine forgiveness of sin ('because in his forbearance he had overlooked the sins of the past', (Rom. 3:25) as the content of God's justifying act.

The reality of sin is, therefore, the theological context for advancing the idea of justification in biblical writings.

This remains the case in the classic disputes of the sixteenth century. Indeed, one striking English example, Richard Hooker's brief treatise on justification, bases itself on an earlier verse from Habakkuk (1:4): 'The wicked doth compass about the righteous: therefore perverse judgement doth proceed'. The sermon involves an exposition of the biblical proposition that *all* have sinned, which Hooker insists must be held literally, against the Roman Catholic opinion that the Blessed Virgin Mary was without sin.[1]

The point that justification implies the reality of sin can also be made conceptually, apart from the interpretation of authoritative texts. The concept of justification implies the contrast between justice and injustice, and within that context, the ethical contrast between good and evil. Theologically, to speak of God's righteousness is implicitly to deny that in him is any unrighteousness at all, neither injustice nor any kind of evil or wickedness. The human situation, however, is characterised by wrongdoing, in terms both of injustice and of moral evil. There is no prospect, therefore, of making sense of justification if we cannot give an account of human sin.

Similarly, and as a direct consequence, it is also essential to offer some account of the idea of human responsibility for sin. Paul puts the argument bluntly in the first chapter of Romans. The suppression of truth, which is what human wickedness amounts to, is culpable for Paul because, 'All that can be known of God lies plain before their [the Gentiles'] eyes' (Rom. 1:19). 'Their conduct therefore, is, indefensible; knowing God, they have refused to honour him as God, or to render him thanks' (Rom. 1:20–1).

That is the reason for human vice, and that is why God's just judgement will stand against such people at the day of retribution (Rom. 2:5). The pains which Paul takes to establish the culpability of all humanity in the face of sin depends on the capacity of human beings to have behaved otherwise, and thus in some sense assumes their freedom. Sin implies guilt; guilt implies responsibility; responsibility implies freedom.

So much is clear from the New Testament texts; but we may well ask how this nexus stands up to modern scrutiny. At a common-sense level it does not fare too badly. Whether it is true or not, people *imagine* that they have individual freedom of their wills. Furthermore, most people have little hesitation in thinking of themselves as capable of doing wrong and occasionally even of admitting that they have done wrong. It is also obvious that the modern public has something of an enthusiasm for the idea that wrongdoers (of certain categories) should be punished. On the face of it, the concepts of sin, guilt, responsibility and freedom are in good health and wide currency.

On the other hand, even slight acquaintance with scientific and philosophical discussion over the past 100 years reveals the pressing claims of determinism and of a mechanistic model of the brain.[2] The prevalence and popularity of the analogy between human brains and computers, supported apparently by the biological science of genetics, suggest that, to at least some degree, human beings can ascribe their alleged faults not to free choice, but to unfortunate pre-programming. On this model the concept of sin looks antiquated and unnecessary. Wickedness is identified as socially dysfunctional behaviour requiring reprogramming by suitable combination of rewards and punishments. Feelings of personal guilt are a waste of time, except in so far as they offer an incentive to redirect activities into socially useful channels. In the end it is impossible to say whether human freedom is real or illusory, and quite unnecessary to decide the matter. Most human beings are programmed in such a way as to give a whole society the incentive to resolve clashes of individual predispositions. The social good is not, therefore, something freely chosen and meritoriously pursued; it is the constantly changing outcome of an instinctive preference of comfort over discomfort. Rational people behave in such a way as to maximise their comfort and prosperity. Societies are human groupings which are constantly renegotiating where the balance of comfort lies, locking up deviants and rewarding those who create wealth and contentment.

As I have suggested, the Christian theological commitment as being a nexus of ideas relating to sin, guilt, responsibility and freedom can still count on widespread popular support. But the mechanistic alternative can view this position with some detachment. It could, after all, be socially useful for people to *believe* that they possess freedom, that doing certain things should be seen as wrong, and that the perpetrators of wrongdoing should be treated as guilty – as long, that is, as what Christians disapprove is broadly conducive to the general comfort and prosperity.

The possibility that this might not always be the case began to appear in the euthanasia debate. The argument in favour of ending the lives of 'useless' people who cost the public purse a lot of money, or the refusal to distinguish between the intention to kill and to relieve pain, even with the secondary consequence of shortening the sufferer's life – both involve challenges to Christian theological traditions prohibiting the killing of the objectively innocent. To kill such people is to commit sin, according to the Christian tradition. In the eyes of campaigners for euthanasia, who suggest that they have widespread popular support, it is hardly sensible to waste resources on 'living vegetables' (note the dehumanising vocabulary), when these could be used to help others who could make a greater contribution to general comfort and prosperity.[3]

The public plausibility and support for such arguments strongly suggest that, beneath an apparent acceptance of the sin-guilt-responsibility-freedom nexus, shifts of considerable importance are underway. The overt defence of the idea of sin by Christian theologians is long overdue – otherwise they will awake to discover that the term 'sin' has been reserved for chocolate cake and the transgression of a diminishing number of sexual taboos; and that their case has gone by default.

At this stage it is necessary to refer to the traditional doctrines of the Fall and of original sin. These received massive attention, especially in English-language theology, following the Darwinian developments of the nineteenth century. Theology had to meet the charge that, if there had been no Adam to fall from grace to sin, then there could be no grounds for speaking of redemption from sin; or at least no restoration of humanity to any mythically-conceived state of pre-fallen perfection.[4] Although that particular objection, once thought to be devastating, has lost its force, there is an aspect of the matter which deserves a great deal more thought than it receives. This concerns the account that is given of the development of the human brain. We are completely familiar with, and have no difficulty with, the legal concept of diminished responsibility. In its popular, non-legal sense this means that we do not consider a person who is mentally ill, or who has an acute learning disability, as incurring the same degree of blame for actions which we would hold to be blameworthy if committed by a fully competent adult. Animals we exempt from blame altogether. They may be naughty, and we may punish them if they impede the orderliness of our domestic lives, but we are conscious of using language analogically if we refer to them as 'wicked' or 'evil'.

So the question arises, at what stage in human evolution would it have become right to speak of 'sin'? The answer might well be, that at whatever stage sin made its appearance, at that moment we might want to speak of the Fall. Sin and the Fall are, in other words, implicates of each other. But can we attach any significance to an idea of 'original sin' as the consequence of the Fall? Here it is helpful to recall that the classic doctrine of original sin spoke of it as incurring both the guilt and the penalty of sin. All human beings are born in sin, and are guilty and punishable because of that sinfulness. The objection to original sin in that sense was that it apparently obliged Christians to believe that millions who had died beyond sight or sound of the Gospel, including babies who died unbaptised, would suffer the penalty due to those who were sinners because of their deeds.

If we refuse to accept that appalling consequence, there seems a good deal to be said for another view – that, when we speak of 'sin' we have to recognise that the social atmosphere into which all human beings are born is poisoned, so to speak, by the consequence of those past decisions of countless others to which we rightly give the word 'sin'. There was a time, or times, when the human brain had developed to the point that a choice could be made which was, objectively, sinful. From that moment, or moments, we could sensibly speak of the social embodiment of the consequence of sin, and of human beings as imbibing those consequences from their very earliest origins. The more precise delineation of such a view would depend on some kind of dialogue with the modern understanding of the human brain, a science which is in anything but a settled state.

It remains to give some account of sin in itself. Theologically it implies a missing of the mark or aim which God gives to human life, and is thus a condition of being in an objectively disordered state. Guilt for such sin has to be distinguished from subjective disappointment at not living up to our ego ideal. As a result of our long process of dependency and nurture through infancy, all human beings carry about with them a self-image which is the result of socialisation. Crucial to our sense of contentment is whether or not (or the degree to which) we have been taught to see ourselves as loveable. To be a sinner is not the same thing as getting ourselves into a situation in which we fear that some significant person in our lives may no longer hold us in esteem. Or we may have suffered extensive episodes of parental or peer disapproval, and as a result internalised their blaming activities as our guilt. Or on the other hand, and perhaps less commonly, we may have been reared in an atmosphere of smothering adulation and consequently resist all assignment of blame as maliciously conceived.

To distinguish between an objective understanding of sin and certain psychologically-induced feelings of guilt is no small project. Nor is it a certain one. Human beings possess different degrees of self-awareness, and differing capacities for self-interrogation. But the Christian disciple surely cannot avoid believing that he or she is capable of sin, and therefore has a duty to identify it in the fabric of his or her life.

What, then, are 'sins'? In various places Paul lists the sins of which human beings are capable. In Romans, for example, we read that when God gives human beings up to their own depraved way of thinking:

> They are filled with every kind of wickedness, villainy, greed, and malice; they are one mass of envy, murder, rivalry, treachery, and malevolence; gossips and scandalmongers; and blasphemers, insolent, arrogant and boastful; they invent new kinds of vice, they show no respect to parents, they are without sense or fidelity, without natural affection or pity (Rom. 1:29–31).

There are other lists, too, in 1 Corinthians (5:10f; 6:9f), 2 Corinthians (12:20), Galatians (5:19–21), Ephesians (4:31; 5:3–5), Colossians (3:5 and 8), 1 Timothy (1:9), 2 Timothy 3:2–5), Titus (3:3) and 1 Peter (4:3). They are also to be found in the intertestamental literature, and in Rabbinic and Stoic sources. These sins are not, therefore, distinctive to Christian scrutiny and identification.[5] What Christian theology did undertake, at a fairly early period, was the codification of seven 'deadly' sins – pride, covetousness, lust, envy, gluttony, anger and sloth (already listed in the writings of St Gregory the Great, Pope from 590 to 604). In St Thomas Aquinas' magisterial treatment of them, they stand for a disordering of a created feature of life, which, if rightly ordered, would lead to human flourishing, both socially and individually.[6]

We may well conclude that, despite the mechanistic account of the brain, there is a strong case to be made for the view that human beings enjoy the kind of freedom to choose which makes sense of the traditional understanding of sin. Sin in the Christian tradition embraces both social and personal wrongs. If the pendulum has swung heavily in recent times to reveal our implication in social disorders – racism, sexism and the oppression of the economically disadvantaged – there is nothing to prevent our also acknowledging that we fall victim to pride, envy and lust. Indeed, we might well claim that one of Christianity's contemporary strengths is its capacity to identify and speak frankly about sin, and to connect its blatant appearance with its proper theological interpretation: missing (or not even aiming at) the divinely offered mark or goal.

To that account we should add a willingness to struggle with the distinction between what is objectively wrong in our lives, and those things about which we merely feel guilty subjectively, then to reconnect objective and subjective guilt, and to confront them with the objective and justifying grace of God. But we need now to consider the next aspect of the context of justification, namely the reality of forgiveness.

GRACE AND FORGIVENESS

In all Christian theological accounts of atonement, whatever may be said about God's wrath towards human sin, and however we may evaluate the respective weight given to God's condemnation or his forgiveness of it, it is axiomatic that God's purposes towards humankind should be identified as gracious. As we have seen from Milton, however culpable human beings may be for their sin, nevertheless God is motivated by his love to come to rescue humankind, and does so at stupendous personal cost. The grievous weight of sin can only be fully measured when we have taken account of the love of God our Redeemer. It is grace which takes the initiative:

> Father, thy word is past, man shall find grace;
> And shall Grace not find means, that finds her way,
> The speediest of thy winged messengers,
> To visit all thy creatures, and to all
> Comes unprevented, unimplored, unsought?
>
> (III, 227–31)

In this (Reformed) account it is stressed that grace comes 'unprevented', meaning that it is by definition 'prevenient grace'; in other words, the initiative in finding a means of reconciliation between God and humanity lies with God alone.

But what do we understand by 'grace', which became, both in the Pelagian controversies of the fourth and fifth centuries, and then at the Reformation, the subject of the fiercest controversy? It is perhaps useful to accept from the outset that grace has no one fixed meaning. But at the same time, one familiar usage might provide a kind of standard against which to measure others – that is, its occurrence in the threefold benediction which closes St Paul's second letter to the Corinthians: 'The grace of the Lord Jesus Christ, and the love of God, and the fellowship of the Holy Spirit, be with you all' (2 Cor. 13:14). The implication is that the congregation should consider themselves upheld, sustained and nourished in a grace, love and common life which is God's personal presence and power among them and in them.

We need not separate grace, love and fellowship, or annex them respectively to Christ, God and the Holy Spirit. 'Grace and peace to you from God our Father and the Lord Jesus Christ' (2 Cor. 1:2) was Paul's opening greeting in the same letter. The phrase 'the grace of our Lord Jesus Christ' is also, we should notice, ambiguous (why should Paul *not* be ambiguous?). Grace could be what Jesus gives or sends; it could also be what he constitutes or is. The term 'fellowship' or 'common life' (*koinonia*) gives us very good grounds for saying that Jesus Christ is precisely God's loving presence with humankind, sharing his risen life with us. We might thus derive what I have called a standard against which to measure the variety of uses of the term 'grace' in other contexts. (For example, in 2 Cor. 8:1, Paul speaks of the 'grace' – rightly translated in the NEB as 'the grace of generosity' – which God has given to the Macedonian churches, a few verses later comes his paean of praise to the 'generosity' of our Lord Jesus Christ in becoming poor for our sake.)

If grace, so understood, is nothing less than God's personal presence, then John Henry Newman was perhaps wrong to formulate the words:

> And that a higher gift than grace
> Should flesh and blood refine,

48

God's presence and his very self,
And essence all-divine.
      (From the hymn, 'Praise to the Holiest in the height')

If grace be measured by the incarnation, there is no greater gift. And one would consequently be rather cautious about phrases such as 'the grace of orders', as though one might have gifts from God which were separate from God himself, or from the Holy Spirit.

To insist on the prevenience of grace is of the greatest importance in establishing what I shall call the 'tone' of faith. Where this insight has been lost in the history of Christianity – not by being formally denied, but more subtly by being overlaid with other ideas or proposals – there the faith has quite markedly changed in atmosphere. Grace and generosity can be readily distinguished from anxiety and mean-heartedness, and there have been, and are, versions of Christian faith which are more redolent of the latter than the former. Grace and generosity elicit gratitude. Again, I believe, we are dealing with an elemental attribute of the tone of Christian faith, a tone which makes so persuasive George Herbert's plea, in his poetic masterpiece, 'Gratefulness', for the gift of such a heart 'whose pulse may be thy praise'.[7] The gifts of God in the creation and preservation of the earth and of humankind are many and various; but gratitude has its standard and norm when we take into account above all (I quote the General Thanksgiving from the 1662 Book of Common Prayer), 'Thine inestimable love in the redemption of the world by our Lord Jesus Christ, . . . the means of grace and . . . the hope of glory' (again, the phrase 'the means of grace' is best interpreted as the personal presence of Christ in the sacraments of baptism and Eucharist).

So conceived, the response of gratitude is inseparable from the gift of forgiveness of our sins. Thus it is completely axiomatic for Paul that Christ died 'while we were still helpless' (Rom. 5:6): 'Indeed, rarely will anyone die for a just person – though perhaps for a good person someone might actually dare to die. But God proves his love for us in that while we were still sinners Christ died for us' (Rom. 5:7; NRSV). The connections between the generosity of this act of love in which God takes the side of guilty sinners, and the outpouring of the response of praise, becomes explicit in Paul's lyrical outburst, beginning with the question: 'Then what can separate us from the love of Christ?', in Romans 8:35–9.

STORY, ATONEMENT AND JUSTIFICATION

We have spoken of the reality of sin and the reality of forgiveness as the sole context in which it makes sense to develop an understanding of justification by grace to be received by faith. It may be helpful here to place the concepts of forgiveness, atonement and justification in relation to each other. To refer back to the analysis of the grammar of story which we used in chapter 1, we might well say that the forgiveness of sin forms one essential part of the *theme* of the story. The *setting* of the story is the whole of God's creation, and that whole creation is seen as, in some sense, dislocated or disordered. If we take the words 'reconciliation' or 'redemption' as inclusive terms, then the forgiveness of sin is part of reconciliation, but not the whole. The *plot* or *plots* of the story then tell how God goes about forgiving human sin by sending his Son to earth 'for us and for our salvation'.

Atonement theory is an attempt at an explanation which arises directly out of the fact that what God did about human sin is both extremely surprising, and gives rise to many questions and objections. Within this context, the word 'justification' draws attention to the fact that God's

actions transfer the sinner from the realm of punishment
and death to the realm of righteousness and life. Justification is achieved by the forgiveness of the sinner's sin.
One may speak of it, therefore, as a resurrection concept.
What is negative in the human situation is exchanged for
what is positive, death for life, hostility for reconciliation,
captivity for freedom, and so forth.

It is the radicalness of the new situation which justifies
speaking of justification as a resurrection concept. Unlike
the equivocal, ambiguous and sometimes partial acts of
forgiveness of which we are capable, God's forgiveness is
radical and complete. He puts our sins as far from him as
the east is from the west (Ps. 103:12). Our experience of
God's forgiveness has the recreating power of the most
complete, generous and thoroughgoing human forgiveness we have ever experienced, and more. In the next
chapter we shall consider the issue of merit, which bears
closely upon the way in which we receive God's forgiveness.
But justification by grace is a way of saying, in a formula,
that atonement is based on God's intention of love towards
humankind. It is the generous beauty of that forgiveness
which creates the unmistakable tone for Christian communities and relationships.

Does the word 'justification' imply or contain a particular theory or explanation of the atonement. It appears
not; rather, it announces a fact resting wholly upon God's
gracious initiative towards sinners incapable of saving
themselves. But at the same time the forensic connotation
in 'justification' suggests the plausibility of the implied
metaphor of a legal process that reverses a 'guilty' verdict
passed against the sinner. It is for this reason that the
sixteenth-century Reformers, who laid such stress upon
justification by faith, came so strongly to develop a forensic
theory of atonement. Prominent in Reformation and post-
Reformation theology is the idea that the sinner is the

subject of God's judicial sentence, that the punishment which is due to the sinner was borne in the sinner's place by the Son of God, and that as a consequence, God the Father accepts the bearing of that punishment as making an equivalent satisfaction for sin, and thus propitiating his just wrath against the sinner. As Milton put it:

> Behold me then, me for him, life for life,
> I offer, on me let thine anger fall.

This penal satisfaction theory of the atonement is different in emphasis from earlier attempts at explanation – for example, from that of Anselm, which became standard within medieval Catholicism. Anselm's account of atonement certainly involves the payment by the God-Man of an unowed debt of self-offering, which God accepted as a settling of his claim upon humankind. What is missing from Anselm, but present in the Protestant theories, is the emphasis upon punishment. This became important to Protestants not just as a consequence of the reading of Scripture; it was the sheer centrality to them of justification by faith which provided the impetus for exploring the forensic aspect of justification by means of the law-court metaphor.

Contemporary defenders of the penal satisfaction theory rightly now speak of the language as metaphorical.[8] This important concession is bound to imply that, in certain respects, the application of a theory of specific penal exchange to the death of Christ is not appropriate to the atonement, and that there remains a dimension of mystery. In other words, the narrative of our salvation is not, in a literal sense, one of penal substitution; by itself the importance to a sound Christian theology of justification by grace to be received by faith does not give such a theology of atonement a normative status.

JUSTIFICATION: JESUS, ST PAUL AND ST JAMES

An undertaking was given at the beginning of this chapter to investigate a problem about the status of St Paul's emphasis on justification, in relation to Jesus' own teaching, in which the concept does not figure – at least, not in the same way. This question arises quite apart from the much-discussed issue of whether justification is as central even to Paul as the Lutheran, and more generally the Reformed, tradition has supposed.[9] On the face of it, there is nothing to correspond in Jesus' teaching to Paul's developed argument on justification. Or so it seems. For some account has to be given of a number of prominent features of Jesus' life and teaching which are obviously connected to the doctrine of justification – such as the emphasis on divine judgement in Jesus' eschatology, his teaching on the forgiveness of sins, his attitude to the law and to purity regulations, and not least both his personal role in relation to the coming of God's kingdom and the importance of his resurrection for the entire way in which the story of the gospels is told.

Eschatology is central to Jesus' teaching. The kingdom is that future age of glory, when God's sovereignty will be revealed in human affairs. Salvation is not a spiritualised matter for Jesus or his hearers. God's kingdom will come on earth, 'as it is in heaven' (Matt. 6:10). A new situation has come about with Jesus' ministry and message, and complacency in the face of it is out of the question. Despite the failures and the opposition he encounters, Jesus is confident that small beginnings will lead to a glorious final outcome. Many of those who might expect to be excluded from participation will be included, and vice versa. There will be a judgement, but the criteria will be radically different from expectations, and the result will be dramatic reversals. Promises are made to the poor, the hungry and the oppressed that their situation will be reversed. Though Jesus saw his own mission as primarily to the Jews and to Judaism, none the less the hope of participation eventually in the kingdom of God was going to be open to Gentiles (Luke 13:28ff).

So far as the forgiveness of sins is concerned, Jesus evidently teaches its immediacy, both in his own authoritative activity and in its nearness to surprising categories of people who might otherwise have regarded themselves as hopeless cases. Whereas in some versions of Judaism, the power of God was only available after extensive efforts at discipline and purgation, for Jesus, 'the model of the disciple is the child, the Publican as opposed to the Pharisee, the man who loses his life, the poor, the forgiven sinner, sitting at table with him'.[10] These examples illustrate the personal qualities of the need for repentance, receptivity, humility – and for learning to forgive, as one is oneself forgiven.

In relation to the law, while it would be an exaggeration to say that Jesus disregarded or opposed it, there is clear evidence that he thought external uncleanness trivial compared with moral defilement, especially in respect of the law concerning ritual impurity (Matt. 15:11; Mark 7:15). He is explicitly within the prophetic line of those who held that cultic acts do not exonerate their performers from the moral demands of God's righteousness. His own actions in cleansing the Temple and in speaking of its destruction raised the sharpest of questions as to his personal authority and the threat he posed to existing arrangements.[11]

Finally, we have to take serious account of the personal claims made, directly and indirectly, by Jesus regarding his own agency in the kingdom, and the vindication of those claims provided by the accounts of the resurrection. Resurrection was an eschatological concept for both Jews and early Christians. To say that Jesus had been raised from the dead was to make an assertion about the centrality of Jesus for God's ultimate purpose and creation.

None of these themes amounts to a doctrine of justification by grace to be received by faith, *expressis verbis*. But we may certainly claim the presence of the raw material for the development of such a doctrine. In the first place, we have God's initiative in Jesus' own ministry. It is an initiative which graciously offers the forgiveness of sins to the outcast; the penitent publican is indeed justified. It puts in a wholly new context a traditional evaluation of the place of the law of Moses. It opens up a potential opportunity for the Gentiles to participate in final salvation alongside the Jewish people. It urgently demands a response of faith and trust, a radical obedience to God on the pattern of Jesus' own self-commitment. Such a life transfers the disciple from death to life, from bondage to freedom, from blindness to sight, from sickness to health; the narratives of healing provide the content of the metaphors of salvation. The Pauline doctrine of justification, therefore, turns out to be no simple innovation, but a transposition of Jesus' own message in a new mode consistent with a fuller grasp of the significance of the resurrection. It is no departure from the message of the gospels for Paul to say that Jesus, 'was given up to death for our misdeeds, and raised to life for our justification' (Rom. 4:25).[13]

Nevertheless, there is a difference to be acknowledged – as will be evident to anyone who studies one of the classic passages on justification, such as that in St Paul's letter to the Galatians (Gal. 2:15–21). Here, Paul is dealing with people whom he believes have destroyed, or are about to destroy, the whole point of the gospel by reintroducing aspects of the law into Christian life, notably the requirement for circumcision. He wants to insist that the only way of living the gospel is to live it consistently by faith. The death and resurrection of Christ are the complete pattern of Christian life. The death of Christ is the end of the law. He gave himself up to death for our sins, to set us free (Gal. 1:4). Because we believe that to be true, our new relationship to God is one of faith.

Everyone starts, Paul insists, at the same place, whether they are Jews or (with gentle irony) 'Gentile sinners'; everyone who has faith has been put right with God. The law will not do it; but faith in Jesus Christ will do it – faith in the one whom God has put forward to be a guaranteed means of salvation.

But there is still sin in the Christian life. Why has that not been abolished, and what are we supposed to do about it? The answer is not that it is the fault of Christ; I have to accept responsibility, after building my life on the gospel, for all that goes wrong. The principle of salvation is: the law is dead, 'I' am dead, Christ lives in me. 'My' life is now lived by faith in the Son of God. The 'I' who is sinner and continues to sin owes nothing whatever to the law. If that were the case, then Jesus' crucifixion would have been for nothing. Paul is very blunt: 'You stupid Galatians! . . . You started with the spiritual; do you now look to the material to make you perfect?' (Gal. 3:1).

Because we are about to consider the Reformation division on justification by faith, it is worth remarking that Luther wrote two commentaries on Galatians, in 1519 and 1535.[14] In both of these, but especially in the second, he adopts and adapts Paul's tone of sharp rebuke and applies it to contemporary controversy. The Roman Church, he holds, is guilty of returning to the religion of law by its emphasis on overt rituals and public penance, and by its introduction (or re-introduction) of preconditions to the work of grace.

There was, of course, a thorough and sophisticated response to Luther, pointing to other parts of the New

Testament which have a strong and positive message about the importance of human co-operative activity in the work of grace. In the light of this controversy it is worth emphasising the consistency of the thought that justification is by grace alone to be received by faith alone, and that 'the only thing that counts is faith expressing itself through love' (Gal. 5:6). It is by faith that we are wholly removed from the deadly illusion that we may achieve our own righteousness. By faith we enter into solidarity with Christ, who died and rose again. Our new risen life is life in the Spirit, and the fruit of the Spirit is love and many other gifts. 'It is by the Spirit and through faith that we hope to attain that righteousness which we eagerly await' (Gal. 5:5). There is no contradiction in a righteousness which is ours through faith, and a righteousness which we await – any more than there is a contradiction between a kingdom in which we participate here and now, and a kingdom into which we shall more fully enter hereafter.

What, then, of the notorious contrast between Paul and James, whose insistence that 'faith without works is dead' ('If it [faith] does not lead to action, it is by itself a lifeless thing', James 2:17) also became an instrument of Reformation controversy? Here again there is no contradiction once we realise that the term 'faith' in James stands for the verbal confession of orthodox belief. The subject of the tongue's capacity for mischief has already been raised in the letter ('If anyone thinks he is religious but does not bridle his tongue . . .', James 1:26). James also draws on the established prophetic tradition of criticising hypocritical displays of religiosity, professing to 'love your neighbour' but showing partiality for the materially rich. It is in this context that he is able to observe the truth that the profession of faith is not invariably accompanied by works of love. James and Paul agree in holding that the real grasp of faith entails dying to sin and rising to newness of life in the Spirit. That there is such a thing as an arrested development in this process is as apparent to Paul as it is to James. The difference between them is perhaps one of theological subtlety: James offers a blunter diagnosis and a prescription of the form, 'Don't be a hypocrite'; Paul attempts, in a different context, to uncover some fundamental errors of teaching and approach.

THE SIXTEENTH-CENTURY CONTROVERSIES AND THEIR AFTERMATH

With these observations we arrive at part of the substance of the controversies which deeply divided Protestant and Catholic in the sixteenth century. The issue between justification and the fruit of the Spirit, or between faith and works, could be formally represented as a discussion on how to relate justification to sanctification.[15] And it would be exceptionally convenient if the whole matter could be explained by exposing a misunderstanding between the connotations of the Greek and Latin verbs for 'justify'. As ARCIC II, *Salvation and the Church*, put it:

> The theologians of the Reformation tended to follow the predominant usage of the New Testament, in which the verb *dikaioun* usually means 'to pronounce righteous'. The Catholic theologians and notably the Council of Trent, tended to follow the usage of patristic and medieval Latin writers, for whom *iustificare* (the traditional translation of *dikaioun*) signified 'to make righteous'. Thus the Catholic understanding of the process of justification, following the Latin usage, tended to include elements of salvation which the Reformers would describe as belonging to sanctification rather than justification. (para.14, p.17)

This was no doubt an element of the situation, but it is important to distinguish between different levels of the controversy, which has a distressing way of reappearing even after allegedly having been resolved.[16]

At *one* level the argument is about St Paul's own concern, which, as we have seen, is centred on God's initiative in establishing righteousness for guilty and helpless human beings. Paul's argumentative energies go into refuting the suggestion that humankind needs the ritual and legal provisions of the law (for example, circumcision) in order to comply with what God requires. After God's decisive and gracious initiative in Jesus Christ, all that is needed is union or solidarity with Christ in his death and resurrection. That is achieved by faith; and from this faith springs the new risen life in the Spirit. Although the Reformers argued that there were parallels between this 'legalism' and the 'ritualism' of medieval religion, in truth Paul's concerns and those which exercised the minds of Luther and his fellow Reformers were fundamentally different. As a result, contemporary theology has little difficulty in giving an ecumenical and non-controversial account of Pauline doctrine; but such an account does not so easily resolve the problem over which the sixteenth century was so bitterly divided.

The *second* level of the controversy specifically concerned the process of justification, an account developed in considerable detail in post-Augustinian Western theology to try and resolve the serious problems about free-will which were the Augustinian inheritance. On this matter there continued to be disagreement between highly competent and influential theologians within the Church, for example between St Thomas Aquinas and Duns Scotus. The latter had taught a process of justification which went somewhat as follows:

1   God, of his grace, gives to the human will a habitual

tendency (*habitus*) in the direction of love towards God and humanity.

2   This *habitus* remains passive and inert unless the human will responds in acts of love.

3   These acts of love, because based on God's initial grace, are meritorious, and by them a person is gradually changed into a righteous person.

4   The righteousness so imparted is closely connected to the system which the Church has been given for sustaining right living: in the first instance baptism; then penance for later sins, arising out of sacramental confession, and restoring the individual penitent to a 'state of grace'.

None of this bears any obvious relation to Paul's concerns except that in Luther's mind it created a devastating anxiety about where a person was in the process, and whether he or she had actually achieved the state of contrition required for the infusion of further grace. Luther thus came to believe that the 'process of justification' he had been taught was analogous to the system of law and ritual which Paul had rejected.

In its place Luther taught that humanity was completely unable to rise to God's grace, and that God himself bestows the gift of faith in Christ. This gift is the imputing to a person of a righteousness not his or her own, what he called 'an alien righteousness'. Because of this righteousness alone a person is saved. It is vital that this principle of salvation is seen to contradict human preconceptions of how salvation could come about. This is the 'folly' of the cross, destroying all human righteousness. Once a person is securely rooted in this faith, however, good works must follow, as fruit from a healthy tree. These good deeds are not the cause of justification, but its consequence. In due course, Protestant theologians were to draw a sharp distinction between justification and regeneration or sanctification. (We shall return to the way in which this argument is currently put to rest.)

There is a *third* level of the controversy about justification, which is perhaps the most difficult to grasp but which is none the less the one which continually gives rise to new unease. In the outstandingly valuable dialogue which has been taking place since 1965 between Lutherans and Roman Catholics in the United States, and which produced a Common Statement on Justification by Faith, issued in 1985, this is spoken of as the 'hermeneutical perspective'.[17] The statement explains the matter as follows:

> This doctrine functions as a critical principle in judging all thought and practice. The central point is that the proclamation of God's grace in word and sacrament is itself the saving event in that it announces the death and resurrection of Jesus Christ. God's word does what it proclaims or, in modern terminology, the gospel message is performative; it effects the reality of which it speaks. The preaching of the Gospel has the force of decreeing the forgiveness of sins for Christ's sake. Like a will or testament, it makes human beings heirs of the promise quite apart from what they deserve. (para.88, p.47)

The reason why this is said to be hermeneutical is that it functions as a critical criterion for everything that is said and done within the Church, where everything by definition must relate to the Gospel of God's saving grace.

> The doctrines of justification, of the word and sacraments, and of the church (which for Luther was a 'mouth house' that exists to proclaim the Gospel) are inseparable. Justification by faith is emphasized not primarily by speaking of the doctrine but by so teaching and acting within the

61

church that Christians are constantly directed to God's promises in word and sacrament from which all else flows. (para.92, p.48)

Of these three levels of argument, it is the last two which continually cause problems, but especially the third. In recent years, very great effort has been expended in bilateral ecumenical dialogues between Lutherans and Roman Catholics to resolve remaining difficulties arising from the explicit condemnation of the Council of Trent of what were taken to be the Reformers' errors and exaggerations.[18] From time to time the disputes come to seem oversubtle, remote and self-perpetuating. But at their heart are complex and important matters, not least the issue of the certainty and security of God's forgiveness. How can that be known, thoroughly and transformingly, but without presumption? The psychologically vital issue of merit, to which the next chapter is devoted, explores this matter. And what account can and should be given of the corporate and public life and character of the forgiven community, with its recognised sacraments administered by an authorised ministry? Forgiveness is not a private matter for lone individuals; it is always personal and relational. But its security and finality rests wholly on the fact that it is rooted in God's forgiving generosity, not in human intentions or actions – though they may be involved.

The importance of justification by grace to be received through faith, as of the whole juridical set of ideas applied to the atonement, lies in the finality of the verdict of acquittal. Something is finished. However much we continue to struggle with sins, perplexities and ambiguities, we know that in our dealings with God our redeemer, revenge, resentment and slavish obligations are not just around the corner. Thank God, in Christ there is a new creation.

3

ooooooooooo

Merit and Reward

In this chapter we shall examine the question of whether human beings contribute anything to salvation, and whether their final salvation is in any sense a reward for their efforts. As a matter of fact, the Christian tradition is more or less unanimously opposed to these views, but the discussion of merit and reward has become so horrendously technical that we are at once alerted to some serious complexities in the subject-matter.

But our proposed angle of approach to these issues requires that we step back a little to review our progress as a whole before taking the next step. In the previous two chapters it has been argued that there is such a thing as 'the story of salvation', and that it is the basis of the Christian account of the atonement. But as we examined that story in Milton's great epic, we discovered that there was great difficulty constructing a single, continuous narrative and remaining true to the implications of the doctrine of the Trinity. There is something to be said for presenting two stories, it was argued, both of which contain nuances important to the truth of what is being conveyed. The second of these stories and the one with which we have the most immediate empathy, is that of Jesus' own voluntary offering of his life to his heavenly Father.

But that story itself is not a single story, for the simple and good reason that we have four gospels. Modern narrative criticism encourages us to see that each of the gospels has its own structure and nuances. (Of course, we can construct a synthesis of these gospels – that was done in the early church by a second-century writer, Tatian, in his *Diatessaron*. But it was always an impoverishment of the richness of the Church's response to Jesus.) In particular, we have four rather different modes of telling of Jesus' way to his passion and death, and four rather different forms of resurrection belief.

Naturally, historical questions arise as to the compatibility of the sequence of events. But those are not the only matters of importance. Of equal significance is the way in which Jesus' identity is portrayed through the encounters he has with various people and groups.[1] These brief and vivid narratives are an essential part of how Jesus' death is understood. Had there been a narrative telling of Jesus' resistance to arrest, cursing of his enemies and forcible protest on his way to crucifixion, nothing would remain of the Christian account of atonement as we know it. Following in Christ's steps, as the writer of 1 Peter makes clear, is based on knowing that, 'he committed no sin, he was guilty of no falsehood' (quoting Isaiah 53): 'When he was abused he did not retaliate, when he suffered he uttered no threats, but delivered himself up to him who judges justly' (1 Pet. 2:22–3).

Not only the passion narratives are important, but also are the stories of healing. This is because they offer such a clear contrast between the state of sickness or disability before meeting with Jesus, and the radically new life after the miracle. John 9 has a delightfully told, ironic story of the healing of a man's blindness, in the course of which the healed man bluntly says to the incredulous Pharisees, 'All I know is this: I was blind and now I can see' (John 9:25). These narratives are also extraordinarily important for understanding the atonement because they illustrate the quality of the new life in the form of a simile; it is like seeing for the first time (and, what is more, a lot of people who claim to see have absolutely no insight into this experience).

Now the complex matter of merit and reward – the subject of this chapter – is frequently treated in the gospels, both in Jesus' healings and also in his parables. There is a classic, abstract formulation of the relationship of grace, faith and works in the letter to the Ephesians, which we shall consider in due course – but there are also common-sense questions which are better handled in narratives. It is nonsense to say, for examples, that the blind man contributed nothing to his salvation. He was told by Jesus to go and wash a paste off his eyes in the pool of Siloam; this he duly did, and was rewarded with the return of his sight. But at the same time, it is clearly God's power which has cured him; on this the narrative is completely explicit (John 9:3). The man contributes his trust and obedience; or rather, he has to trust just enough to do what he is told, to follow a prescribed way.

What are Christians saying when they deny that they have any power of themselves to help themselves? These words are used in a collect from the Church of England's 1662 Book of Common Prayer: 'Almighty God, who seest that we have no power of ourselves to help ourselves.' Collect for the second Sunday in Lent). As we shall see, sometimes the English text of these prayers, where they are based on a Latin original, has been given an extra twist in the direction of the Reformation understanding of justification. But in this case the Latin is much the same ('O God, who seest us to be destitute of all virtue'. Both versions are expressions of helplessness; both sound distinctly negative, even depressed.

There is something disgusting about grovelling. 'I cast myself entirely upon your mercy' may be an honourable phrase, and it can be uttered without paroxysms of self-denigration; but there is a way of behaving in the context of human helplessness which is irresistibly reminiscent of the contemptible belly-crawl of a wretched dog to an overbearing master. Is it spiritually healthy, this denial of our capacity to help ourselves? Common sense can readily assent to the idea that God makes the first move in initiating justification. But common-sense has very great difficulty in assenting to the idea that there is absolutely nothing which human beings contribute by way of response. The doctrine of complete helplessness before God begins to look somewhat disgusting. It seems to depict human beings as scarcely recognisable creatures of God, even within the context of the Fall and sin, and God as tyrannical, arbitrary and overbearing. After all, if God merely chooses that one person shall respond and then enables the response to take place; and then chooses that another person shall not respond, and eternally punishes the lack of response – the resultant picture is of a cosmic monster. The issue of human merit concerns the quality of God's justice. It is integral, therefore, to a discussion of justification – and it was deeply controversial at the Reformation.

There are two ways of tackling the question of merit. The first is to return to the Reformation controversies in all their complexity. The second is to confront the actual problem for Christian living. Experience suggests that there is usually a real human difficulty at the root of the arguments about how to interpret the Scriptures, however technical these arguments have become in the course of Christian history. The nexus of issues related to merit is part of a vital human sense of justice and appropriate reward. It also belongs to a fundamental system of gift-giving and exchange, and as such concerns the very roots of human culture, and of how we conduct ourselves as human beings in relation to one another. The vital question here is whether the divine-human relationship is to be seen as totally other than human interrelationships. But at this degree of abstraction, we would do well to begin with an illustration.

As a student I paid a month-long visit to an Arabic country, in the course of which I walked regularly through the Kasbah or market. When the time came for me to go home, I began to inspect the wares on display with an eye for some souvenir presents. As I looked round one shop, crammed with Bedouin artefacts, the shop-owner sat me down, ordered coffee, and began to pull out some of his treasures.

My means were limited, and I was by no means confident of my ability to conduct the appropriate bargaining process in French. But we got on well, and began talking of this and that, when I had the idea of explaining that I was looking for a present for my (then) girlfriend. And because I was lonely and wanted some kind of reminder of her, I took out my wallet where I had a photograph of her. There was nothing suggestive or improper about it, but she was wearing a bathing costume. The reaction was extraordinary. He immediately produced a broach of old Bedouin silver, gave it to me and absolutely refused to take any payment for it. I cannot now recall how I eventually got out of the shop. I *hope* I bought something. But the man's response of giving me a valuable gift in return for my showing him a photograph of my girlfriend made a very profound impression. His reaction was based, presumably, on the fact that to him, my innocent gesture was an act of extravagant, even reckless generosity.

On reflection I realised that what had begun as one kind of exchange, with the rules of which I was familiar – namely the exchange of a commodity for a sum of money – developed rapidly into another kind of exchange with which I was almost completely at sea. I say 'almost' because

I at least had the wit to perceive that it would have been insulting to insist on paying for what the shop-keeper was intent on giving me. I had given an unsought gift by showing him a photograph. He responded with a different gift, equivalent but not the same; he was a debtor to me, and the silver brooch was a partial pay-off of the kind familiar within friendship.

The introduction of the terms 'debt' and 'friendship' at this point illustrates the importance of the idea of gift-exchange for Christian theology.[3] The stories of the gospels are a vital resource in finding our way through the relevant questions. The ingratitude of the servant forgiven a massive debt by his master is one of the most powerful of Jesus' parables relating to forgiveness (Luke 7:36–50). And it belongs to the heart of the mystery of Christian disciple-ship that we are accounted no longer as servants, but as friends (John 15:14f). Moreover, within the debt of human friendship, there is something for the debtor to do. There is a vital question to be asked, if we are to construe the discipleship of faith aright: whether the reciprocity even of unequal human friendship carries over into the divine-human relationship of grace.

We can take a further step into this problem with a psychological observation. Within certain kinds of self-abnegation there is a barely concealed vein of pride. George Herbert closes his book of poems on the Church with a dialogue poem entitled 'Love III'. In it a 'courtesy-contest' takes place between a guest invited to a banquet and the host, whose name is Love. The guest draws back, accusing himself of unsuitability on account of 'dust' and 'sin' – mortality and sinfulness; and a series of exchanges takes place in response to these continued protestations of unworthiness. It is brilliantly crafted to expose what one commentator has aptly called the arrogance implicit within the humility, which refuses to accept Love's gift of 'bearing the blame', or which when eventually persuaded, insist ostentatiously on not coming to sit at table, but being ready rather to serve.[3] The denouement, which has more than a hint of exasperation at the earlier exchange of sophisticated banter, is expressed in a series of unmistakable monosyllables:

> You must sit down, says Love, and taste my meat.
> So I did sit and eat.

It is not in the least fanciful to trace in this poem the impact of Herbert's knowledge of the 1552 Book of Common Prayer, whose Eucharist he knew and celebrated as parish priest at Bemerton, near Salisbury. That liturgy is full of the need for self-examination and of expressions of unworthiness. But in the end the guest is a partaker at the Lord's Table, not an observer. The guest simply has to do what is commanded, to sit and eat in the presence of the divine Host who has accomplished all that is necessary to reconstrue the unworthy and graceless guest as a friend. Acceptance of that new status proves to be the real internal struggle. Protestations of unworthiness, appropriate at one stage, become inappropriate at another.[4]

Herbert's poem is not merely psychologically impressive; it exposes unresolved depths within and below the formal acknowledgements of our unworthiness. For example, it is not unusual to regard the acceptance of the call to be ordained as a pinnacle of self-commitment to Christ. Yet not only does ordination bestow a certain measure of status and security, it is also only human nature that ambition within the clerical profession is not thereby eradicated. While expressing the most fervent abnegation of all merit in God's sight, it is a common matter of clerical self-knowledge generally to reckon oneself worthy of a better niche than one currently occupies. Partiality when making judgements in our own case is so potent a phenomenon, as

Joseph Butler observed in the eighteenth century, that no sooner have we severed one offshoot of ambition, than the monster grows another. This is edifying from a man who, when offered the impecunious see of Bristol, remarked that it was 'not very suitable either to the condition of my fortune or the circumstances of my preferment' – it is a relief to hear him spoken of as 'almost prodigal' in his charitable generosity as the eventual, fabulously rich Bishop of Durham.[5]

So difficult is it to get out of our minds and souls the idea that we have deserved such-and-such a mundane reward for our efforts, that there is something to be said for open light-heartedness about natural ambition as an antidote to hypocrisy. Protestations to the effect that we are helpless and unworthy can become ambiguous, and there is a residual question of spiritual importance about recompense for effort. This psychological fact about humanity, I believe, underlies the continuing importance of the Reformation debate about merit, which on the face of it has been reasonably happily resolved.

THE VOCABULARY OF MERIT

There are no uses of the word 'merit' in the Authorised Version of King James. Even the Latin term *meritum* occurs only three times in the Vulgate, each in verses in Ecclesiasticus or Sirach (that is, in the so-called deutero-canonical literature). One of these passages proves to be important in that it directly expresses the terms of God's final judgement:

> Great as is his mercy, so also is his chastisement;
>> he judges a person according to his or her deeds.
> The sinner will not escape with plunder,
>> and the patience of the godly will not be frustrated.

He makes room for every act of mercy;
everyone receives in accordance with his or her deeds.
(Sirach 16:12–14, NRSV)

Here the Greek, *kata ta erga autou* ('according to one's deeds'), is translated into Latin as *secundum meritum operorum suorum*; that is, the word 'merit' has been inserted, so as to render the clause, literally, 'according *to the merit* of one's deeds'. At once it becomes apparent that we need not look for frequent occurrences of the word 'merit' in Hebrew, Greek or Latin, because there are numerous passages where God's judgement is said to be according to human deeds, in both Old and New Testaments.[6] 'For he will repay according to each one's deeds', is St Paul's own statement on the matter in Romans 2:6. Perhaps most striking and puzzling of all is the text of Romans 2:13: 'For it is not the hearers of the law who are righteous in God's sight, but the doers of the law who will be justified'.[7] How are all these passages to be evaluated, and how are they to be connected, if at all, with the doctrine of justification by grace alone, to be received by faith alone?

The theological basis for ascribing merit solely to Jesus lies in the coinciding of an emphatic denial and a major affirmation. The denial we have already examined – namely a denial that salvation is gained by the works of the law (Gal. 2:16). The affirmation concerns the richness of the work that Christ has carried out. God, 'who is rich in mercy', has brought us to life with Christ, 'so that in the ages to come he might show the immeasurable riches of his grace in kindness towards us in Christ Jesus' (Eph. 2:7). All this is the gift of God, not the result of works (Eph. 2:8f). This language gave rise, in Latin liturgical tradition, to frequent use of the term 'merit' of Christ, both in exalting his merit and denigrating – or even annihilating – our own. The Reformation doctrine of justification by grace alone seized on this tradition and strengthened it dogmatically.

This process of reinforcement is visible in the 1662 Book of Common Prayer, for example in the collect for the twelfth Sunday after Trinity: 'Pour down upon us the abundance of thy mercy; forgiving us those things whereof our conscience is afraid, and giving us those good things which we are not worthy to ask, but through the merits and mediation of Jesus Christ, thy Son our Lord.' There is a change here from the Latin collect. This reads (in address to God): 'Who in the abundance of thy fatherly love exceedest both the merits and the desires of thy suppliants', asking him to 'confer the things which prayer does not presume to ask'. The contrast is not absolute; it is rather one of emphasis.

More obvious still is the change in the collect for the first Sunday of Lent. Where the Sarum Missal had prayed, 'Grant to thy family that what it strives to obtain from thee by fasting, it may carry out by good works', Cranmer paraphrased as follows: 'Give us grace to use such abstinence, that our flesh being subdued to the Spirit, we may ever obey thy godly monitions in righteousness, and true holiness' (1549; 'motions' in 1662). Here it is clear that the idea of obtaining anything from God by fasting has been deliberately suppressed. In five other collects a reference to the merits of Jesus Christ is introduced where the source had none (Easter eve, Easter 1, Whitsunday, Trinity 13 and St Luke's day). The point of these alterations is to stress that the right of access to the Father is solely through the merits of the death of the mediator, Jesus Christ. In fact, to say 'through Jesus Christ our Lord', is shorthand for 'through the merits of Jesus Christ our Lord'. To assert this positively is to imply the negative – that our access to God is not a matter of what we have deserved by our own effort. It is due entirely to grace; that is, the personal presence of God in Jesus Christ, who is the sole ground of our intercession. But grace has to be received by faith. What are we to say, then, of faith?

IS FAITH A WORK?

The question about the nature of faith gets drawn into the discussion of merit for good reason. Common sense suggests that faith is the response of some human beings (but not others) to the claims of Christianity. Faith comes about when someone puts his or her belief and trust in Jesus Christ. The Fourth Gospel says: 'To all who received him [that is, the Word of God], who believed in his name, he gave power to become children of God' (John 1:12). To 'receive' and to 'believe' are active verbs, and their subject is human beings. Receiving and believing are, therefore, things which human beings do. Is faith not, then, a human work?[8]

We can formulate this question at the same time as insisting that God's grace initiates the whole process. By this account, faith is a response to what God has done for human beings in his own self-revelation. The common-sense solution does not appear to undermine the prevenient grace of God.

But supposing we wanted to strengthen the doctrine of grace by insisting that the response of faith itself is a gift: 'No one can come to me unless drawn by the Father', says Jesus in the Fourth Gospel (John 6:44). There is, moreover, the predestination and calling of the elect to consider. 'Those whom he foreknew he also predestined ... and those whom he predestined he also called; and those whom he called he also justified' (Rom. 8:29f). Christ chose us, says the writer to the Ephesians, 'before the foundation of the world to be holy and blameless before him in love' (Eph. 1:4). Or, again, we are paradoxically told to work out our own salvation with fear and trembling, 'for it is God who is at work in you, enabling you both to will and to work for his good pleasure' (Phil. 2:13).

These are the merest snippets of biblical doctrines. But, taken together with a very strong affirmation of human depravity and helplessness, the actual awareness of the nature of 'faith' might well involved no human effort or co-operation of any kind. This is the teaching of famous words from 'Rock of Ages':

> Nothing in my hand I bring,
> Simply to thy cross I cling,
> Naked, come to thee for dress;
> Helpless, look to thee for grace;
> Foul, I to the Fountain fly;
> Wash me, Saviour, or I die.
>   (A.M. Toplady, 1740–78)

But then emerges a paradox. Our salvation seems to depend on the realisation that we are unable to save ourselves. From such vanity we must constantly be delivered. This sense, attitude or experience becomes the precondition of salvation. But how is it to be sustained? Perhaps only through repeated reminders and self-admonitions, accompanied by acts of verbal self-abasement. But is that not, then, a new attitudinal 'work'? Are we not engaged in a constant exercise, somewhat contrary to nature, of squeezing ourselves into nothingness? Is not this all an elaborate effort at producing a set of emotions? Does not faith, therefore, despite protestation, become in the very act of protestation, a subjective work? And is it not, moreover, the very epitome of self-absorbed subjectivism?

This criticism is important because it bears precisely upon the ambiguity inherent in all protestations of human helplessness and unworthiness – an ambiguity which has already been noted. The core of the difficulty lies in focusing exclusively on the human, psychological aspect of faith, as though it were a matter of getting our attitudes right. To be sure, faith has a psychological aspect, because it occurs within human beings. People who are psychiatrically ill sometimes (though not always) suffer hugely distorted 'faith' profiles. Even within the bounds of what is reckoned to be normality, individual psychology can play a significant part in faith's orientation, as many studies have shown. But that is not the end of the matter. Faith needs another explanation, if we are to grasp its nature.

Let us examine the proposal that faith for the Christian is *par excellence* resurrection faith. A feature of the New Testament is that it provides us with an extraordinarily full picture of those who were unpersuaded by Jesus and the apostles. Although written from the standpoint of faith, and for those who were believers, the documents openly acknowledge that not all who heard believed. When Mary Magdalene, Joanna, Mary the mother of James and other women first told the apostles of the empty tomb and the vision of two angels, their words 'seemed like an idle tale' (Luke 24:11). Faith is being defined by its antithesis, namely doubt. St Paul has doubt in mind when he confronts those who say that there is no resurrection from the dead. In that case, he asserts, 'Your faith is futile, and you are still in your sins' (1 Cor. 15:17); 'If for this life only we have hoped in Christ, we are of all people most to be pitied' (1 Cor. 15:19). The reference to sin obtrudes into the flow of argument, but it returns in the end. The undoing of the power of death in the resurrection of Christ is liberation from sin and the law: 'The sting of death is sin, and the power of sin is the law. But thanks be to God who gives us victory through our Lord Jesus Christ' (1 Cor. 15:56f). This demonstrates why it is appropriate to treat justification by grace to be received by faith as a resurrection concept. It is though grace alone, that is the personal

75

presence of God in the risen Jesus Christ, that we are able to escape from the death-dealing grip of sin and law; and the only means is faith in Jesus Christ, crucified, risen and ascended.

But resurrection is, in the New Testament, also an eschatological event. Faith in the resurrection must, therefore, participate in some way in the last things. It is, as St Paul asserts, the present possession and enjoyment of ultimate victory over death through union with the last Adam who 'became a life-giving spirit' (1 Cor. 15:45). This present possession is more than a belief that we will participate in Christ's ultimate victory. It is a connection and a construction of the whole person into a new reality, so that the being of the Christian is a new creation in Christ. Faith, then, is the power which enables us to participate in Christ; it is a 'power at work within us' which is 'able to accomplish abundantly far more than all we can ask or imagine' (Eph. 3:20).

In terms of the narrative or story concept which we have proposed earlier, we can say that a Christian is someone who has understood the ending of his or her life-story, so that all present experiences have been re-orientated to this new ending. It is like discovering that, though I am at present a lowly commoner, in the end I will be crowned as the sovereign. The image of entering upon an inheritance is prominent in the letter to the Ephesians. 'In Christ we have obtained an inheritance' (Eph. 1:11); the Holy Spirit is the 'pledge of our inheritance' (Eph. 1:14); we should have the spirit of wisdom and revelation so that we might perceive 'the riches of his glorious inheritance among the saints' (Eph. 1:18); God has made us alive with Christ, and 'raised us up with him and seated us with him in the heavenly places in Christ' (Eph. 2:6).

This discovery is a mental event, and thus has a psychological aspect. But the claim made for faith must be stronger than that. It is a claim about the nature of human beings in time, and about time itself. We are invited to assent to the view that human beings are not simply bounded by their life-span, nor that time is simply an inexorable process in which the generations rise and fall. Human beings are made for God, and are orientated towards participation in God's kingdom. Faith is the realisation that this is so. It is not to be seen primarily as an effort, but as a discovery. Faith is not, therefore, a work (even though it remains true that as a mental event it has a psychological aspect). It is being present when a revelation takes place.[9]

It is, therefore, entirely appropriate to speak of faith as a gift or calling of God. It is intelligible why the one who is Lord of time could be said to have predestined those who are to be justified. It is not something of which a person can be proud, as though it were an achievement (though psychologically, as we have seen, there is not much to be said for constant efforts at self-denigration). On the contrary, the response to having made the discovery might well be, rather, wonder and gratitude, followed by a burning desire to share the insight of faith with others. The question of those for whom this discovery does not take place is a matter which we will deal with in chapter 6.

WORKS, MERIT AND SALVATION

It is a pastoral commonplace that people will ask, 'Why me?', when afflicted by a grievous illness or accident. They are assuming that the outcomes of individual lives should exemplify an approximate justice between moral effort and reward. This, after all, is the elementary system taught to most children: bad children are punished, and good rewarded. Good children are not punished for the mischief of the bad, or vice versa – not, at least, if a parent or adult wishes to retain a reputation for fairness and impartiality. It is not surprising, therefore, that God's justice comes into question when precisely these situations arise in human affairs. Naïve though the objection may be, it is very deeply laid in human experience.

There are two possible responses, and both are important. The first is the Christian claim that God's gift of life is to the human race as a whole, and that as a whole life is experienced as more positive than negative. The scale of rewards can diminish to the point where (at least from the standpoint of the better-endowed) they appear to have vanished entirely; but still human beings cling tenaciously to life, and receive benefits sufficient for them to continue the struggle. Most people do not commit suicide. From that unsurprising fact we may conclude that for most people, the balance of the verdict is that living contains more positive than negative aspects. This argument deserves a better hearing than it commonly gets, so wedded are we to evaluating life on the basis of individual lives. But all our lives are part of a social web. Even if individually my life has very little to commend it, I pray that under circumstances of suffering I might have the grace to see that my endurance might eventually confer some future benefit on others.

The second response to the objection, 'Why me?', is altogether more subversive. Again from the Christian point of view, we have to consider the nature of the link between praiseworthy individual moral effort and the reward of protection from illness or accident. Moral behaviour or the performance of religious duties places God under no obligation to recompense the individuals concerned, according to Christian teaching. At this point all that has been said about grace becomes relevant. For grace means that God has already done all that is necessary to establish his justice in the divine-human relationship – at the discovery of this enables me to reclaim my life as one who is forgiven. Grace is a resurrection, a being raised with Christ; and then life may be lived in the assurance that nothing whatever can separate the believer from God's love. The guarantee applies to all accidents or illnesses. These occur, but within a new justice-context. Nothing we have done can possibly place God under an obligation to protect us – and likewise, nothing that happens to us can be construed as evidence that he has simply abandoned us to chaotic chance, the slings and arrows of outrageous fortune.

We could ask why, once this guarantee of inseparability from God's love has been received, we should not simply cut loose from all moral effort and sin boldly. It may be that this was a solution which appealed to certain early Christian, or Christian Gnostic, groups, who opted for licentiousness as a proof of their indifference to the world. (It may also be that they were the subjects of malicious misrepresentation.) But there is a counter-intuitive ring about the question. We are invited to suppose that the grateful recipients of God's gracious forgiveness of their sins are, the next moment, going to forget all moral effort and bask in the sunshine of divine approval. This simply sounds an implausible combination of attitudes. Those who truly have no intention of expending any effort to live a good life seem more likely to have been the victims of self-deception in their original gesture of repentance. True repentance implies a lively self-awareness; and self-aware-ness guarantees the need for future contrition and amendment of life. That is no more than ordinary Christian experience.

Justification, therefore, delivers the believer into the realm of sanctification. The two are inseparable: 'two aspects of the same divine act'[10] Sanctification implies the effort of good works, beginning with proper attempts at self-examination, repentance, contrition, recompense (if appropriate) and amendment of life. The goal of sanctification is full eschatological redemption – in a word, the enjoyment of heaven. But the mention of heaven provokes a new question. Does not the promised reward of heaven motivate the effort involved in sanctification? Are we not back in the whole schema of reward for accumulated merit? But this is, so to speak, an optical illusion – the result of looking at lives from what might be called the biographical perspective. From this viewpoint, all we see are simply unfolding events as a given individual strives to realise his or her life-goals; at the end of this process is the reward and ultimate enticement of eternal life. But if we substitute the eschatological perspective for the biographical one, we see that everything we engage in is wholly conditioned by the miraculous and gracious gift of final redemption, of justification by the atoning death of Christ. As a consequence, all manner of effort is subsumed within the overarching response of gratitude, for the gift of the world, of life and of the world's redeemer. Moral effort and striving are restored to human experience, but in a new key, with a new tone – one which is wholly consistent with the foundational resurrection act of justification by grace.

This I take to be the significance of the words in Ephesians 2, which are classic for the discussion of merit and reward:

> For by grace you have been saved through faith, and this is not your own doing, it is the gift of God – not the result of works, so that no one may boast. For we are what he has made us, created in Christ Jesus for good works, which God prepared beforehand to be our way of life.
>
> (Eph. 2, 8–10, NRSV)

To be created for good works in Christ Jesus means that the whole concept of a created order, into which humanity fits, has to be christologically conceived. When we do 'good works', they are ones which God has 'prepared for us to walk in'[11]. They amount, in other words, to a fulfilment of the basic ground-plan of human capacity and aspiration, and they are simply conducive to individual and social human flourishing. Such deeds are, therefore, abundantly worthy of our efforts, as a response of gratitude to the one who is the giver of the whole of life.

In a certain sense, therefore, we may say that there are rewards for good works, and some passages in the New Testament seem to imply a certain proportionality – big rewards for big efforts, more modest ones for lesser achievements. It is almost as if, once the main question has been decided – whether or not we have passed the final judgement – it becomes a matter of fine discrimination whether the examiner awards a first, second or third class degree. Language of this kind is essentially pictorial, as is St Paul's image of building on a foundation with gold or silver, or even with hay or straw: 'If what has been built on the foundation survives, the builder will receive a reward. If the work is burned, the builder will suffer loss; the builder will be saved, but only as through fire' (1 Cor. 3: 14–15, NRSV). Other pictures are much more subversive, as in Jesus' parable of the labourers in the vineyard in Matthew 20: 1–16. Here, expectations of proportionate justice are overthrown by an eccentric landowner who indulges lazy latecomers with extravagant generosity. We may notice, incidentally, that the final reward is fixed in advance for the virtuous (who are the focus of the parable, and thus the analogue for the intended audience). It is generally those who reckon themselves virtuous who have such difficulty with disproportionality and sheer grace.

Theologians have frequently been tempted to radicalise the divine-human relationship by saying that it contains *no* element of reciprocal gift-giving. But that would be to overlook creation. To be a creature is both to be the recipient of a gift, and to enter a relationship of indebtedness to the creator – an indebtedness which elicits from us a sense of the appropriateness of reciprocal gift-giving. But the fact is that what we naturally offer in response to God is distorted by sins, ambivalence and a certain, even comic, inadequacy. The best of which we are capable still falls short of the glory of God. It is in this context of *aporia* that God gives yet again, and this time supremely of his own being, his Son, to be way, the truth and the life. In the Son, we are acceptable. And having entered a new system, so to speak – a system not of strict reciprocity, but of friendship and loving mutuality, in which going into debt is allowed – we find an almost unimaginable generosity in operation.

Ordinary Christian life is lived somewhere between these two systems. Reciprocity of relationship the merits-reward scheme, is impossible to remove from our heads; indeed, it can become the occasion for understanding a little of God's incredible generosity in giving himself, in Jesus Christ, unto death. Once we see that we have entered into the mutuality of love through grace – an entry which is made by faith – it does little harm to allow the old system of merits and rewards to provide us with a spur. All we can do is grossly inadequate when compared with what has been done for us. We are invited to do what we can; and we do it, conscious of a certain comic disproportionality of scale.[12]

4

ooooooooooo

Salvation and other faiths

As for all the gods of the heathen, they are but idols:
but it is the Lord that made the heavens. (Ps. 96.5)

The opening of a magnificent Hindu temple in London
in the mid 1990s was accompanied by processions
through the streets of what were called 'idols'. It was start-
ling to hear a term, so full of negative connotations in
Jewish, Muslim and Christian contexts, used positively,
both by the media and the worshippers themselves. In a
Protestant culture, of course, idol-worship was a charge
laid against the Roman Catholic and Orthodox Churches.
Considerable care and subtlety has gone into the distinction of grades of devotion accorded to the saints and in
their representations wood, stone, plaster and paint – as
distinct from the worship of the one true God. Idol-worship
is, for all Christian traditions, as for Jews and Muslims,
simply forbidden:

They have mouths, and speak not:
  Eyes they have, and see not.
They have ears, and hear not:
  Noses have they, and smell not.
They have hands, and handle not;
  feet have they, and walk not:
  neither speak they through their throat.
They that make them are like unto them:
  and so are all such as put their trust in them.
                              (Ps. 115:5–8)

83

A well-honed insult.

A little reflection tells us that the ancient people of Israel had real grounds for their hostility. They were a small, intensely embattled nation surrounded by large and predatory neighbours. Conquered and scattered into exile, they feared for the very existence of their faith. Nor was revulsion from the beliefs and rituals of other religions always misplaced. Human sacrifice and sacred prostitution were among religiously sanctioned ways of achieving a people's prosperity. And the Old Testament provides plenty of evidence that some Israelites were attracted to, and adopted, the local deities. In the face of an internal threat of syncretism or outright apostasy, the psalmist's judgement was heartfelt: 'Confounded be all they that worship carved images, and that delight in vain gods: worship him, all ye gods' (Ps. 97:7). And devout men and women, raised in the Christian tradition, have embarked on heroic missionary expeditions equipped with little more than that understanding of the religions they were about to encounter, and hoped to supplant.

A COPERNICAN REVOLUTION?

A modern writer was not, therefore, exaggerating when he called for a Copernican revolution in the way that Christians regarded other faiths, especially those generally known as world religions (there are religions which are local, not world phenomena). Taking as his premise the view that Christian faith could not be the only doorway to eternal salvation, John Hick argues that the great world faiths are all part of the self-disclosure of the divine. The different religions have differing names for God:

> But what we cannot say is that all who are saved are saved

by Jesus of Nazareth. The life of Jesus was one point at which the Logos – that is, God-in-relation-to-man – has acted; and it is the only point that savingly concerns the Christian; but we are not called upon nor are we entitled to make the negative assertion that the Logos has not acted or is not acting anywhere else in human life. On the contrary, we should gladly acknowledge that Ultimate Reality has affected human consciousness for its liberation or 'salvation' in various ways within the Indian, the semitic, the Chinese, the African . . . forms of life.[1]

This proposal has been very intensively and extensively discussed, as one would expect, in the last 20 years.

The roots of what Hick himself calls a 'pluralistic' view of salvation go considerably further back in time. In the 1960s the World Council of Churches set up a department of Dialogue with People of Living Faiths and Ideologies, whose director – Stanley Samartha of the Church of South India – made notable contributions through consultations and publications.[2] The 1960s also saw a watershed in Roman Catholic teaching on other religions. *Lumen Gentium,* a document of the Second Vatican Council, asserted:

> Those also can attain to everlasting salvation who through no fault of their own do not know the gospel of Christ or His Church, yet sincerely seek God and, moved by grace, strive by their deeds to do His will as it is known to them through the dictates of conscience.[3]

Behind this consensus lies a considerable discussion, vivid since the Columbus' discoveries in the fifteenth century of untold millions of people living and dying without sight or sound of the Church. The same problem had been thoroughly and wisely considered in the Protestant world at the first World Missionary Conference in Edinburgh in 1910. A Commission of that Conference, devoted to considering the status of other faiths, wrote of the harm that had been done in India by missionaries who lacked the wisdom to appreciate the nobility of certain aspects of Hinduism.[4]

But the first sophisticated attempt at a Christian theology of other religions is to be found in the writings of Friedrich Schleiermacher (1768–1834), who has acquired the title of 'father of modern theology'. Schleiermacher was a German Protestant pastor who became the most famous theologian of his day. Educated within Pietist circles, he responded warmly to the broad philosophical and religious culture of the German enlightenment and romantic movement. In a unique early synthesis of theology and psychology, he sketched a theory of religious consciousness which in effect provides a Christian-based theology of the religions. The religions, he held, are diverse ways in which 'consciousness of God' is socially organised around their own particular 'essence', or core principle. Some religions are more admirable than others, and Schleiermacher did not hesitate to assert the superiority of the essence of Christianity. This essence, he believed, provided not merely the core principle of the Christian religion, but also a way of accounting for the plurality and diversity of other ways of responding to the divine.[5]

Schleiermacher never acquired a profound knowledge of other religions. Judaism was the only faith practised on any scale in Germany in his time, and Schleiermacher's view of its popular (as distinct from its philosophical) form was regrettably contemptuous. But the stress he laid on the way in which human beings experience the divine, as well as religious doctrine and ethical teaching, has proved important and suggestive. It is notable, for example, that John Hick speaks of the effect of Ultimate Reality upon human consciousness. Moreover, most Christian attempts

to construct a theology of other religions try, as did Schleiermacher, to identify a unifying principle to interpret their
plurality. The relationship which that principle of unity
has to Christian doctrine and practice is another question.
It is a further question whether salvation can be attained
from within another religion – and if so, how the grounds
of that salvation relate to the atonement.

AN OLD QUESTION, A NEW CONTEXT

For our own orientation upon those urgent questions, let
us take a strong view of the catholicity and apostolicity of
the Church. Where John Hick simply abandons the classic
christology of the creeds as parochial, I propose to take as
axiomatic the view, explicit in the letter to the Ephesians,
that it is God's will, 'that the universe, everything in heaven
and on earth, might be brought into a unity in Christ,'
(Eph. 1:10). The universality of Christ is the basis for
the catholicity of the Church. God has put all things in
subjection to Christ, 'and gave him as head over all things
to the church which is his body, the fullness of him who
is filling the universe in all its parts' (Eph. 1:22). These
doctrines, we should notice, were advanced long before
the Church had any kind of social status, let alone domi-
nance, and were believed and proclaimed in the context
of a riotous religious pluralism. They are bold convictions.

The apostolicity of the Church is the similarly bold conviction of the presence of Christ in the task of going to all
nations and making them his disciples, baptising them in
the name of the Father and the Son and the Holy Spirit,
and teaching them to observe all his instructions (Matt. 28
19–20). God has entrusted his Church with the ministry
of atonement, having reconciled the whole world himself
in Jesus Christ (2 Cor. 5:19). The theology of evangelism
will concern us in greater detail in chapter 6 – but for the

moment, we assume the traditional evangelistic imperative of the Church. Together with these classic doctrines, we remind ourselves of the approach to the atonement taken in this book. According to this view, the New Testament does not contain one normative theory of the atonement, but presents a family of narratives of salvation arising out of different idea-complexes. All of these, in different ways, give rise to questions, and the labour of theory formation is designed to give coherent and convincing answers to these questions, and so to reduce surprise. Some questions are internal to the Christian system, in that they presuppose that God does indeed save those who put their trust in him. Other questions are external to the system, asking, for example, whether it could possibly be consistent with ordinary justice if only those who put their trust in Jesus Christ are saved.

Thus, the issue we are raising about salvation and other religions is a genuine one, and needs an answer. It is a question which arises directly out of the narrative of salvation. If sin is the context of justification, as we have argued, there is no way of avoiding the question of whether sinners who have not turned to God for forgiveness through Jesus Christ are saved. All the four idea-complexes which lie behind attempts to offer a theory of atonement imply the seriousness of the human condition. Adam's disobedience led to his expulsion from the garden and condemnation to toil, pain and death. The slave is excluded from the inheritance of the master. The guilty criminal is condemned and imprisoned for his or her wickedness. The cultic guilt of the worshipper entails exclusion from the community. None of these accounts creates a presumption in favour of salvation by any other means than Christ's atoning death.

Furthermore, the explicit teaching of St Paul, who considers the status of Gentiles in the first chapter of his letter to the Romans, is to the effect that there is no natural righteousness in humanity. Ever since the beginning of the world, he argues, God has made himself known through his creation. Evil conduct is therefore indefensible in all, as is failure to honour and thank God for his goodness and generosity. Gentiles and Jews, he continues, are in the same situation, all alike 'under the power of sin' (Rom. 3:9); and sin brings death. The preaching of the Gospel reveals the human condition for what it actually is. The teaching is anything but optimistic. But does it therefore follow that other religions are nothing but diverse forms of idolatry? On idolatry, St Paul is again quite explicit. He condemns the folly of exchanging 'the glory of the immortal God for an image shaped like a mortal man' (Rom. 1:23), or of offering 'reverence and worship to created things instead of the Creator' (Rom. 1:25). But can we still ask whether there could be no non-idolatrous content to other religions? The question is real, and has a new context. A plurality of faiths and philosophies is not in the least a modern circumstance – yet it is modern to have the size and age of the earth in mind as we pose the question. The results of geographical exploration in the fifteenth and sixteenth centuries, and the cosmology and palaeontology of the nineteenth and twentieth centuries, were certainly not known to the biblical writers. We are entitled to ask whether every form of religion now known to humankind necessarily falls under St Paul's swingeing condemnation.

We remind ourselves of the confident voice of a certain kind of orthodoxy, cited by a modern Roman Catholic who proposed to dissent from it: 'It cannot be doubted [said the sixth-century St Fulgentius of Ruspe] that, not only pagans, but also all Jews, heretics and schismatics, who are outside the Catholic Church, will go to that eternal fire which has been prepared for the Devil and his angels'.[6]

This form of rigorism eventually led in the twentieth century to an official denial. Father Leonard Feeney, who was in charge of a centre for Roman Catholic students at Harvard University, persisted in defending three lay teachers at Boston College, sacked for maintaining that all those not expressly members of the Catholic Church would be damned. The row lasted from 1949 to 1953, when Feeney was himself excommunicated. There is an irony as well as a tragedy in being excluded from the Church for maintaining that those outside the Church are debarred from salvation.[7]

PLURALISTS, EXCLUSIVISTS AND INCLUSIVISTS

The question, then, is new and complex, and has been extensively and intensively discussed. One influential way of organising the disparate material is in three groups or paradigms of response, labelled respectively pluralist, exclusivist and inclusivist.[8] These, it is said, are characteristic of the Protestant discussion, though the last two have featured also in Roman Catholic writing.

A *pluralist* is impressed by the evidence for historical and cultural relativism, and does not believe that Christianity can claim a wholly unique status among the world religions. Furthermore, a pluralist is likely to argue either that there are many equally salvific paths to divine reality, or that the interaction of religions will, in due time, lead to a new form of world faith. John Hick is on his own testimony a pluralist of one kind or another, but there are earlier examples – notably the German philosopher and theologian, Ernst Troeltsch (1865–1923).

An *exclusivist* maintains the uniqueness and finality of Christianity; there is no alternative stance for a Christian than to proclaim salvation through the atoning work of Christ. The cross stands in judgement on all forms of religiosity. A Dutch missionary, Henrick Kraemer (1888–1965) is usually cited as an example of a typical exclusivist, precisely because he is sharply critical of the new pluralist proposals. To affirm that there is 'no salvation outside the Church' is, of course, exclusivism; but it is notorious that what counts as 'the Church' is capable of elastic interpretation and redefinition.

Inclusivism is a certain kind of middle way. A Scottish missionary, John Farquhar (1861–1929), for example, argued as long ago as 1913 that Christ was the crown and fulfilment of Hinduism. Therefore the relationship of a Christian missionary to the Hindu faith and philosophy is not that of a zealous opponent of idolatry, but of one who is trying to identify the aspirations and aims of Hinduism as a constructive preparation for the Gospel.[9] A distinguished modern Roman Catholic, Raymond Pannikar, goes so far as to call himself a Christian and a Hindu.[10] Many Roman Catholic theologians, who redefine 'the Church' to include people of goodwill following the dictates of their conscience, believe themselves able to synthesise the classic exclusivism of the tradition with the demands and challenges of a modern understanding of other faiths.

It would be immensely convenient if this threefold typology clarified the issues involved. But '-isms' frequently promise more than they deliver, and cover up important differences with generalisations. Add to that the fashionably overused and under-examined concept of the paradigm, and you have a recipe for confusion. The Church of England Doctrine Commission report, *The Mystery of Salvation*, while agreeing that the terms exclusivism, inclusivism and pluralism have performed a useful function, argues as follows:

> At their best, they remain ambiguous, and are places on a spectrum, rather than separate opinions. At worst they can

91

label people, often in a judgemental way ... We find ourselves moving beyond any of these three positions; indeed,
it may be that our statements can be found to give support
to all three at various points.[11]

One other general term ought to be mentioned at this
point, namely *universalism*. This is generally defined as the
doctrine that every human being will come to enjoy
the benefits of salvation in due course, and that none can
be finally lost in everlasting damnation. This is a quite
separate view, and is compatible, in theory at least, with
pluralism, exclusivism and inclusivism as presented above.
The question of whether all will be saved is not identical
to the question of whether there are many paths to salvation. A pluralist is not necessarily also a universalist; there
might well be those to whom the path to God or Ultimate
Reality has been revealed, but who refuse to take it. But
universalism also raises serious questions which will be
discussed in chapter 6.

FIVE THESES ON OTHER FAITHS

A Christian can only approach a person of another faith
on the basis of respect for difference and a desire to
understand. Careful study of the beliefs of other faith-
communities has a role to play in the development of such
respect, because individual believers may make mistakes
about their own religion (one need only think of the
millions of half-instructed Christians). But the encounters
in which Christians are really interested are personal, not
institutional. Formal dialogues may make a contribution
to education or social relations, but they can also have the
effect of blocking genuinely personal meetings.

What follow are specific recommendations to Christians
as they meet with people of other faiths. 'Faiths' is not

here limited to any strict definition of religion or religious communities. Many Westerners today have tentative and informal allegiances to a variety of belief-systems, held, as it were, experimentally; among them is respect for the ancient goddess, Fortuna, in the forms of fatalism and astrology. These half-entertained beliefs are often combined syncretistically with remembered or socially conveyed elements of Christianity, or with any other religion found attractive. New Age beliefs are also included. Above all, it is not intended to define a (rarely specified) elite league of 'world religions', as though Christians might talk in an educated voice to Muslims, but with condescending sympathy to Aborigines or American Indians.

THESIS 1: *God does not bring millions of human beings into the world to damn them eternally.*
It is important to affirm this belief, because the converse has been in the past confidently, or apparently confidently, asserted, as we have seen. A moving story is told about an early Zulu convert who was in agony over the fate of his parents, having been assured by an evangelist that their damnation was certain. Why, he kept asking, did not God send the missionaries sooner?[12] When someone told the Sikh convert, Sadhu Sundar Singh, that his mother would go to hell if she did not become a Christian, he replied, 'Then I will ask God to send me down to hell so that I may be with her there'.[13]

This preliminary denial (of the teaching that those who have never heard of Christ are eternally damned) is also important because it bears upon personal anxieties and motivations. Roman Catholic teaching did not clarify the matter until the twentieth century, and its clarification is still resisted in certain strict evangelical circles.[14] Although to one way of thinking the denial has the ring of self-evident truth, the grounds for it need to be expounded and defended.

How can it be known that God does not create human beings who perish without hearing the Gospel, and are then punished for their sins? An atonement theology, we have argued, has to offer a reasonably consistent construal of God's intentions and actions. This is not for the sake of theory alone, but because the imitation of God is a practical aim of Christian ethics. The slaughter of the innocents is a particularly telling example. When Herod, on hearing of the birth of the Messiah, ordered the massacre of all boys aged two years or under in and around Bethlehem what moral consistency could there be between the supposed motive for the incarnation and the fate of the children, if it were taught that those children were damned? (Infant damnation was assumed on the basis of the doctrine of original sin, according to which both the guilt and the penalty of sin were passed at birth to each human infant.) If God were capable of dealing with human beings like that, so were (and are) human beings capable of dealing thus with each other. Conversion at the point of the sword could easily be justified, and was indeed practised. If a person refused baptism, it was argued, then they were likely in God's judgement to have been condemned, and so could be dispatched from life without guilt. The doctrine and the practice cohered.

It may be said that the argument for imitation is fallacious; that God is not an agent in a narrative, and that his standards of justice are strictly unknown to us. But even allowing for that, the very affirmation that God is good constrains the way in which we may construe his actions. If God behaves like Moloch, and we know Moloch's behaviour to be evil, it will not be possible to say that God is good. God's behaviour cannot be that of a petulant or callous tyrant.

The precise form of the thesis we are discussing is a denial; and the denial does not imply that God saves all humankind, which is the contention of universalism. It states rather that all who are not explicitly Christians or members of the Church are not therefore damned, nor do they necessarily perish as though they had never been.

There are further implications to be drawn from the grounds of the argument we have advanced. It will not do merely to say that the fate of those not knowing the truth is unknowable, as though they might as well be damned *en masse* as saved. The proposal simply to be agnostic about their destiny refuses to accept the moral force of the case. God's action, in the incarnation, for the salvation of humanity must be consistent with his treatment of million upon millions of human beings, what we now know to be the vast majority of humankind.

But why is it that so many Christians have believed what St Fulgentius so bleakly expressed? The moral content of the argument gives us an insight into this complex matter. Moral systems have indisputably varied over time – especially as regards what counts as justice – and still vary between cultures. The Scriptures as a whole do not present a single, fully articulated theory of justice. Different standards are evident at different stages of Old Testament history; and the New Testament, while appealing to God's justice or righteousness, does not give it a precise social form. It does not explicitly teach, for example, the normativeness of the distributive justice characteristic of modern democracies.

The Scriptures do contain, however, explicit illustrations and condemnations of gross tyranny, sufficient to provide a kind of minimal or universal morality, applicable in many different social and political situations. The history of theology has plenty of examples of arguments, not just about justice in societies, but also about what may justly be attributed to God. What we may say about Fulgentius, as about Augustine, is that their status as saints does not imply their infallibility. The doctrine was wrong in its own times, and might well have been criticised by other contemporary Christian theologians.

There is a methodological argument relating to this question. Whereas within the tradition, both single texts and unexamined philosophical premises have often played a disproportionately large role in predetermining the outcome of an argument, what is specifically proposed here is the fundamental character of narrative. God's being is identified not by a collection of single verses containing references to his specific attributes, nor by imported philosophical tenets of a metaphysical kind, but by the force and quality of a series of narratives in which he is an agent. In these, his character and intentions come to expression. We may say, for example, that the story of the slaughter of the innocents, which is told with explicit sympathy for the mothers, does not require us to import a doctrine of divine foreknowlege and predestination. We can simply assume the inconceivability of God requiring their sacrifice and subsequent damnation, on the basis of the central theme of the narrative in which God is active for human salvation.

THESIS 2: *We may have confidence that God's judgement of non-Christians is just, wise and merciful.*
The overwhelming consensus of scriptural narratives is that there is a resurrection to judgement. This is summed up in the credal sentences, 'From thence he shall come to judge the quick and the dead' (Apostles' Creed), and 'he shall come again with glory to judge both the quick and the dead' (Nicene Creed). The judgement scenes depicted in the Scriptures have notoriously variable content. But one vivid illustration of common belief is contained in the first letter of Peter. The author congratulates his churches

on having turned from their pagan past with all its 'reckless dissipation'. Their former partners in these immoral activities now abuse them:

> But they will have to give account of themselves to him who is ready to pass judgement on the living and the dead. That was why the gospel was preached even to the dead: in order that, although in the body they were condemned to die as everyone dies, yet in the spirit they might live as God lives.
> (1 Pet. 4:5f)

Post-mortem judgement provides Christians with 'the sense of an ending' so vital in the formation of narrative.[15]

Within that narrative God's role is just, in the sense that wickedness will receive its deserts, but also generous and surprising as the vivid parable of the sheep and the goats in Matthew 25 makes clear. Jesus, after all, came to seek and to save those who were lost. He minds about minorities – the one sheep or the single outcast. He overturns the mighty, who generally control the scales of justice in their own favour. In the judgement of such a God we may have confidence, in the sense that hypocrisies and disguises will be swiftly penetrated, and hesitant goodness will be identified. Above all, we may have confidence that God desires our salvation. At the point of public absolution, the 1662 Book of Common Prayer reminds the penitent that they are dealing with a merciful God, 'who desireth not the death of a sinner but rather that he may turn from his wickedness and live'.[16]

THESIS 3: *All religions are open to demonic distortions.*
This again has the ring of self-evident truth, as we contemplate well-known evidence – not least from the history of Christianity itself. Christians have also to be aware of a romanticism which, on the basis of very little experience, is readier to credit the idealistic self-portraits of other faiths

than it is to take seriously the claims of our own. And religious motivations are not to be underestimated. When religions appeal to divine instruction or will, they offer a most potent form of legitimation. They can create martyrs in unjust causes; they can justify terror and oppression; they can exonerate from blame those who, by ordinary humane standards, are guilty of horrendous crimes. The religions of humankind, we have every reason to think in the late twentieth century, are dangerous.

In many cases, we only need minimal human values to perceive the negative developments within a religion. But the implications of the potential for distortion are important. Because religions can go wrong, we are bound to be open to criticism. And the criticism for which we are ready internally can also be applied externally. If, for example, we are critical that authoritarianism within the Christian faith can undermine human responsibility, we may well be alert to the same negative actuality in the context of another faith. Of course, it would be prudent first to consider the complexity of another belief-system, and its mode of internal communication, before leaping to conclusions. Even within the Christian faith, different denominations develop idiosyncratic ways of conveying and decoding messages, which outsiders find puzzling. There is no easy way in which religious language can be compared, contrasted or equated in different religious systems. This does not mean that an outsider can understand nothing: merely that he or she should not leap to negative conclusions. But criticism is a possibility, and even a duty in some circumstances.

It was in the context of dispute and separation between Christians of different convictions that the author of 1 John instructed his friends not to trust every spirit, but 'to test the spirits, to see whether they are from God' (1 John 4:1). Three tests are proposed: the acknowledgement of

Jesus, the recognition of the writer's authority, and love for fellow-Christians. A Christian who is meeting people of other faiths is obliged to test the spirits and, without ignorant insensitivity or undue speed, is bound to use similar criteria.

THESIS 4: *We must be open, in humility, to the possibility that God is at work in other faiths.*
Nothing that has been said in exposition of the Jewish, Christian and Muslim view of idolatry needs to be withdrawn, for it still to be the case that idolatry does not constitute the whole content of other faiths. Some faiths permit no physical images. But even if idolatry were defined as the worship of false gods, it could still be consistently condemned without allowing that other religions consist of nothing but false devotion.

Moreover, there is a strong strand of traditional Christian teaching which insists that Christians too have a struggle against false devotion, a struggle within themselves to worship, honour and obey but one God, the one true God. This was Luther's view, and there have been many whose personal spiritual pilgrimage has confirmed its truth.[17] 'As a rule', said H.R. Niebuhr, 'men are polytheists'.[18] The implications of this are far-reaching. For if it is possible that a grasp of the truth could be mixed with falsity and error in the understanding and practice of a Christian believer, why should it not be the case in a member of another faith-community?

We have already defined 'other faiths' as including many Western semi-pagans. It is often plainly the case that elements of Christian belief still persist in such people, and there are many examples of admirable lives lived from the resources of Christian examples and standards of earlier generations. That is not, however, the precise claim of this thesis, which refers not to residual Christianity, but to goodness and holiness of divine origin within the lives of people wholeheartedly living within the context of another faith. This means that the complex of attitudes and virtues, which for Christians count as sanctity, are in evidence outside the Christian faith. Should this surprise us? If we needed an explanation, might we not say that the Holy Spirit is active within creation and is by no means a prisoner of the Church?

If the question be put as to whether people of other faiths are saved by this saintliness, no answer can be given. No one is saved, we can be certain, by the performance of a certain number of good works. Indeed, an aspect of that same saintliness would be its liberation from that kind of legalism. The reason for giving no answer is that we do not and cannot know whom God saves. There was once a fervent discussion between Christians about which truths it was necessary to believe if a person were to be saved. That discussion ended when it was firmly pointed out that God alone knows any particular person needs to believe in order for him or her to be saved. Roman Catholic theology also developed the useful doctrine of 'invincible ignorance'. You could not reasonably require someone to believe truths of which they were invincibly ignorant; and there was an appended discussion of the great variety of degrees and types of 'invincibility'.

We should therefore be open, in humility and love, to the possibility that God is at work in other faiths. This is consistent not merely with a critical view of other faiths, as of our own, but also with a firm denial that God saves people because they are sincere in what they believe.[19] Dreadful things are believed with sincerity and passion. Nor would we be committed to the view that there are many ways of salvation, as the doctrinaire pluralist would hold. It is, indeed, paradoxical that the pluralist is obliged to deny to all the religions their own specific claims to uniqueness, and to construct a higher religion which all who wish to be reckoned as tolerant ought to profess. And it is ironic that this new superior belief is often formulated by a Western intellectual convinced that he or she is resisting Christian imperialism.

THESIS 5: *A Christian may none the less have complete confidence in wholeheartedly embracing the faith and commending it to others as true.*

The theological basis of the practice of evangelism will concern us in chapter 6 of this book. The thesis is listed here because of its relevance to the attitude that a Christian brings to meetings with people of other faiths.

A personal encounter convinced me of its importance. I was in conversation with a Jewish woman, who was strenuously objecting to the practice of Christian evangelism. After clarifying my own opposition to disgraceful or manipulative methods of evangelism, I admitted to my own hope that she might one day come to acknowledge Jesus. She was incensed and affronted. I asked why, and was given a long explanation of the oppressiveness of all systematic belief-systems. Her view was, in fact, a philosophical exposition of certain features of post-modernism. I then asked why she was trying, with some passion, to convince me of the truth of her own arguments, even though these were not the religious content of Judaism. The discussion ended without capitulations on either side. But it seemed, and still seems, odd to me that anyone should believe the tenets of a modern philosophy more passionately than believing in his or her own faith.

My conclusion is that I can see no reason why an orthodox Trinitarian Christian should not enter into a personal discussion of matters of faith, open to God's Spirit in the other person, intelligently and humbly ready to learn, and capable of self-criticism, but none the less hoping and longing to be able to do some small justice, in word and deed, to the richness of God's love and of the inheritance of faith made available in the Church of Jesus Christ; and in this way, offering Jesus' invitation to come to him.

∞∞∞∞∞∞∞

The parable of the ring in Lessing's *Nathan the Wise*

From time to time, it occurs to us to wonder whether we would hold the views we do had we been born in another time or place. The thought is absurd because (so far as we know) personal identity is wholly particular. I am the one person I am; 'I' am not a possible other. Transmigration of souls is the theory which seeks to give an account of alternative personal identities. But these views are rather like imagining or dreaming that we are dead: we have to be alive to dream it. I have to be the 'I' I am in order to imagine the oddity of being another. Otherwise we might just as well be thinking of two entirely different people.

All the same, the thought disturbs. Is there not a connection between the fact that I was born to Christian parents in a Christian country and my present Christian convictions? If we observe the ground we occupy from a little way off, we see from that standpoint that very large numbers of equally convinced Muslims, Jews, and so forth, likewise have backgrounds in their own faith-communities. It is disturbing to think that all our most convincing reasons for holding our faith may be no more than the rationalisation of inherited prejudices. The same thought applies to our social and political convictions; but in the case of

103

religion, the claim to truth is sharper and more exposed
– and, perhaps, more fragile.

Some people, of course, are converted to another faith.
They thus make a personal decision which has the hall-
mark of apparent authenticity. Not for them a merely
inherited set of doctrines and practices. Unfortunately this
gives us no clear indication of truth, because there are
conversions in all possible directions. Moreover, people
have a disturbing tendency to be converted to another
creed or faith found within their societies, sometimes as a
result of unsatisfactory personal experiences within their
native religion. Christians in England become Hindus;
Hindus in India become Christians. Though members of
a given religion love to read stories of conversions to their
own faith, or denomination within a faith, the observer
merely notes the occurrence of a few exceptions to the
rule, amounting to no overall pattern.

Perhaps the observer wants to claim that the only reasonable conclusion is that none of the religions are true; that
the one detectable pattern is of lapsing from the practice
of religion altogether. As soon as people start to think
deeply about cultures and how they reproduce themselves,
they cease to ascribe absoluteness to their own faith. It is
a tempting thought which occurs to most of us at some
time. To lapse has the attraction of apparent authenticity,
if we have been brought up within a faith-community. We
can boldly decide to lapse, and thus revolt against
inherited convention. The only problem is that this view
itself becomes an inherited convention, in which a lot of
people are brought up. What protects it from its own
criticism?

We must conclude, with some relief perhaps, that no
faith or philosophy of life can be untrue merely because
we have been brought up in it. At the same time, the
thought disturbs. Does not the fact that I have been

brought up in a certain way of thinking impose on me a particular obligation to review it critically, lest I should be guilty of unthinking prejudice? To test it against other beliefs, to prevent my being blind to weaknesses and even falsity in its arguments? A view of this kind would apply to all positions, including the standpoint of the observer – who turns out to be standing on no superior platform at all.

Needless to say this discussion is familiar in modern theology and has created a vast literature. The problem is known as relativism, and is particularly associated with the name of Ernst Troeltsch (1865–1923).[1] But it has very much deeper roots. It is the subject of a beautifully told parable in *Nathan the Wise* (1779), a play by the writer and philosopher, G.E. Lessing (1729–81). The parable has its own complex pre-history in the work of Salomon Ibn Verga (a fifteenth-century Jewish doctor), in Boccaccio's *Decameron* (1348), and more remotely still, in the work of Moses Maimonides (1135–1204), whom Lessing had read in his youth.[2] Precisely because it is in narrative form, it is well worth careful examination.

The story is told by Rabbi Nathan in the course of a discussion about the religions with Sultan Saladin (the historical Salah-el-Din, who lived from 1138 to 1193). In far-off times, a man came into the possession of a beautiful opal ring which had supernatural power to make whoever wore it, in faith:

gain favour
In the sight of God and humankind.
(line 1915f, with an explicit reference to Luke 2:52).

Naturally he wore it always, and bequeathed it to the son whom he loved the best on condition that he, in turn, would do the same. Possession of the ring conferred the status of seniority in the household, irrespective of birth. This tradition was faithfully observed for generations.

In time, the ring was passed to a man who had three sons who were equally dutiful and whom he loved equally:

> By loving weakness he was led
> To promise it to each of them in turn.
>   (1938f).[3]

But when he came to die, the man realised that two of them would be grievously disappointed. So he sent for a jeweller and had two other rings made which were identical to the true ring in every respect. Even the father could scarcely distinguish them. He gave one to each son privately with his blessing, and died:

>   Scarcely had
> The father died, than each comes with his ring,
> And each one claims to be the master of
> The house. There are enquiries, arguments,
> Complaints. In vain. There was no power to prove
> Which ring was true ...
>   Almost as hard as now
> For us to prove the one true faith.
>   (1958–63)

Saladin protests that this does not solve his question, because the three religions are manifestly distinguishable from each other, even down to food and clothing. Nathan disagrees. What is the basis of our convictions? he asks. It comes, surely, from our parents, who from childhood gave us many proofs of love and who never deceived us:

> Can I believe less in my ancestors
> Than you believe in yours?
>   (1984f)

So he returns to the parable. The three sons appealed to

law, and swore to a judge that each had received his ring from the hand of his father. None of them believed that the father could play him false. Rather than malign his father, each with regret was bound to believe his other brothers were deceivers. The judge replied that, if the father himself could not be called into court, then he declined to give a final verdict. But he was prepared to put a test to each of the brothers. He had heard of the power of the true ring 'to make beloved' its wearer. So, he asked, which of the three was loved best by the other two? On getting no reply, he concluded that all the rings must be false. Perhaps the father had lost the real ring and had had three counterfeits made.

Then the judge offered his advice on how to behave in this situation of radical uncertainty:

> Let each believe for certain that *his* ring
> Is the original ...
>   Let each one strive to emulate
> His [the father's] love, unbiased and unprejudiced.
> Let each one of you vie with the other two
> To bring to light the power of the stone
> In his own ring. And may this power be helped
> By gentleness, sincere good nature,
> Charity and deepest devotion to God
>   (2034, 2041–7).

The judge finishes by modestly adding that, in a thousand thousand years, a wiser man than he might in due course be able to give judgement.

Does this parable illuminate the situation between the religions? One objection could be that the dilemma was caused by the father's weakness, his unwillingness to favour one son above another, and his readiness to deceive rather than to accept responsibility for his actions. He loved his children, and because he himself wore the ring, his children presumably loved him. He must, none the less, have foreseen the arguments and impasse to which his action would give rise after his death. He stands accused of cowardice in refusing to observe the conditions on which the ring was given to him, preferring dissension after his death to tension before it. Had he thought carefully, he would have perceived that ownership of the true ring would make its wearer loved and held in honour; discord, therefore, could have been avoided in the end. The father's example is hardly a reputable analogy for God's ordering of the world.

The objection sounds reasonable as far as the doctrine of God is concerned, at least from a Christian standpoint. But the parable unerringly pinpoints the difficulty in the Christian narrative as it stands. It is said that God loves humanity; that he loves so much, indeed, that he sent his only Son for our salvation. Why then did God not make that way of salvation unmistakably clear? If salvation was so important, if the alternative to it was damnation, would not a loving God have ensured that the one and only way was completely distinguishable from all false substitutes? The parable of the ring is at its strongest precisely in relation to the state of practical uncertainty in which the brothers are obliged to live. They have no immediate access to their father's motives. He could not be summoned to testify. We, the hearers of the parable, have privileged access given us by the author of the parable. But in the case of the differing religions, there is no authorial voice.

In this situation of uncertainty, the judge's interim solution is impressive. He does not know for certain which ring is true, or even whether all the rings may be false. He is in no better situation than the brothers. But on the presumption that the claim of one brother is true, and consistently with the power of the ring, he advises them to show the richest form of love – gentleness, sincere good nature and devotion to God – of which any or all of them is capable. In this way, we the audience, who have privileged knowledge that one ring is indeed genuine, are given a kind of assurance that in due course, in the very long run, the real situation will become clear. In the mean time, nothing whatever is lost by living in love and gentleness.

This is a parable of some subtlety, functioning on a number of different levels, as we see the dilemmas of the brothers, of the judge, and of ourselves as spectators of the drama. To hear these voices as a convinced Christian is to recognise the difference between practical certitude and absolute certainty. God himself has denied humanity the kind of self-evident certainty attaching to sense-experience. Though I may claim to know God as certainly as I know my own existence, I cannot claim that know-ability as public knowledge. In my relationship with others, therefore, I have to take seriously the fact that what seems evident to me is not evident to them – and through no fault of their own. They cannot be compelled to consent to my way of seeing things, on pain of not being taken seriously.

I have, moreover, to accept that from another person's point of view a discrepancy may arise between the content of what I claim to know with certitude, and my behaviour towards them. If I claim knowledge of God's love, but treat my fellow human beings dismissively, aggressively or manipulatively, at once the consistency of my faith is open to question. The key to this matter is attentiveness to particularity. The intimacy of God's love is composed of his minute attentiveness to the details of who I am, combined with his love and fidelity. God calls me by my name; God does not categorise me. There is a humility and a gentle-ness in this attentiveness which I dare not deny to my fellow human beings of other faith-communities. I am not asked to deny my convictions, or to hold them merely tentatively. It is precisely because of my convictions about the person God that I am called to approach other people with gentleness, sincere good-nature, charity and deepest devotion to God. The matter will be clearer in God's good time.

5

∞∞∞∞∞∞∞

The Sacraments and last things

THE CHURCH, THE SACRAMENTS AND THE STORY OF SALVATION

In the grammar of narrative which we set out in chapter 1, there were four elements to be discerned occurring in sequence: a setting, a theme, a plot (or plots) and a resolution. In the Christian story of salvation, the resolution comprises the contents of eschatology, that is the resurrection, last judgement, heaven and hell, and the new creation. In the Nicene Creed the final clauses state: 'We believe in one holy catholic and apostolic Church. We acknowledge one baptism for the forgiveness of sins. We look for the resurrection of the dead, and the life of the world to come.'

Our attention now switches from the *setting* and *theme* of the story, and away from the presupposition of the plot, or plots, to focus on the resolution or goal which is the outcome of God's gracious work in Christ. This outcome is 'the life of the world to come'. The subject has already arisen in our discussion. Justification, I argued, is a resurrection concept: it accomplishes the transference of the person who has faith from the realm of death to life – and in this context, 'life' means eternal life which is victorious over death. Human death is not, therefore, the end: it is not able to separate us from the love of God which is in Christ Jesus our Lord (Rom. 8:39). This perishable body

111

must put on imperishability, this mortal body immortality. And as a result, we may commit ourselves to work steadfastly for the Lord, because in that resurrected, victorious Lord our labour cannot be in vain (1 Cor. 15:58).

Despite the credal narrative sequence of the Church, the sacraments and eschatology, the fact is that the Church can become virtually invisible in the narrative – until, that is, we recall that members of the Church are narrators of the story. This does not imply that the Church is its inventor: she does not bring the story into being. But the Church does bears testimony – a testimony which is the explanation for the very existence and confidence of the narrators. Rather as the authorial voice disappears in a well-crafted novel, so the Church may become invisible in the story of salvation. None the less it is also true that the Church instantiates or embodies the latest episode of the story, which is remembered and told, not for its own sake, but for the sake of her next actions. The Church lives, so to speak, out of the capital of her memories and her hopes, which she keeps in currency by the very act of telling the entire story of salvation, from start to finish.

The doctrine of the Church, however, does not enjoy universal esteem. I recently invited a group of Anglican clergy to search their memories for the teaching they were given in theological college about the Church. It was an instructive exercise. Some could remember nothing whatever. Some even doubted whether the subject was in any way important. The only person upon whom the teaching had made a profound impression had been educated theologically as a Baptist. The force of the analogy between a husband's love for his wife, and Christ's love, nourishment and tender care for the Church (Eph. 5:22–33); the election of the Church in Christ, and the role of the Church as the agent of Christ's reconciliation of all things to himself on earth and in heaven (Col. 1:15–20) – these themes had been entirely lost.

But to reclaim the biblical teaching about atonement and justification implies taking seriously the role given to the Church as the fore-ordained bearer of testimony to God's grace, herself loved by God as the bride of Christ, and her destiny being in due course to be presented to Christ 'in splendour, without a spot or wrinkle or anything of the kind' (Eph. 5:27). We are tempted to judge our own experience of the Church in a similar way to the Victorian spectator of Sarah Bernhardt's riveting stage-portrayal of Cleopatra: 'How unlike the home life of our dear Queen'. But the result of refusing to confront the challenge of a Church which might, in God's sight, be holy and without blemish (Eph. 5:27) is either a spiritual failure to accept her vocation, or too great a willingness to accept a dualistic idea of individual salvation separate from the salvation of the whole body.

The point may be made in another way by observing the dénouement of the Gospel of St Matthew. Here, the risen Jesus claims that all authority in heaven and earth has been granted to him, and that as a consequence, the eleven disciples are to 'make disciples of all nations, baptising them in the name of the Father, and of the Son and of the Holy Spirit, and teaching them to obey everything that I have commanded you'. And, he adds, 'Remember, I am with you always, to the end of the age' (Matt. 28:19 NRSV). The 'you' of that statement is the Church, who baptises and with whom the risen and ascended Lord persists. In the Gospel of John this persisting presence is spoken of as the help of the Advocate, the Holy Spirit, whom the Father sends in the name of the Son, and who reminds the Church of the teaching of the Son (John 14:26). Or again, in the Gospel of Luke, the connection between the ascension of Christ and the sending of the Holy Spirit is

113

made absolutely explicit: 'I am sending on you the gift promised by my Father; wait here in this city until you are armed with power from above' (Luke. 24:49). Pentecost, as described in Acts 2, is the direct fulfilment of that statement.

To speak of the atonement without speaking of the Holy Spirit in the Church is a serious theological deficiency. It was identified as such in a powerful early twentieth-century monograph, *Atonement and Personality*, by an Oxford Anglican theologian, R.C. Moberly:

> The relation of what he [Jesus] did to us, its working, its reality for and in us, you can only explain at all in terms of Pentecost. An exposition of atonement which leaves out Pentecost, leaves the atonement unintelligible – in relation to us. For what is the real consummation of the atonement to be? It is to be – the very Spirit of the Crucified becomes our spirit – ourselves translated into the Spirit of the Crucified. The Spirit of the Crucified, the Spirit of him who died and is alive, may be, and please God shall be, the very constituting reality of ourselves.[1]

What is at issue here is a genuinely Trinitarian theology, in which one does not separate the work of Christ from the work of the Spirit. We shall shortly see how important is the theme of power, alike for atonement and for an understanding of the Church and sacraments.

Another early twentieth-century voice of importance, P.T. Forsyth, a Congregationalist, insists: 'To enter Christ is in the same act to enter the Church which is in Christ. Faith in Christ is faith in One Whose indwelling makes a Church, and Who carries a Church within His corporate Person.'[2] It is specifically in relation to the Church that we see the closeness of the work of Christ and of the Holy Spirit. Atonement is not an event for its own sake, but for the sake of life and fellowship with God. At

114

the heart of that life lies worship; and all worship is in the Holy Spirit.

So the introduction of baptism into the discussion is no intrusion into the previous account of God's grace and of the faith which justifies. It is not presented as a kind of consequence to be solemnly enacted, once all the right faith conditions have been established. Rather, just as the Church needs to be visible because she is the presupposition of the event of any kind of narration, so baptism and Eucharist must allotted the status given them in the New Testament as integral to the ordinary life of the faith-communities. Social anthropologists tell us that rituals generally precede the elaboration of doctrine.

None the less the books of the New Testament, especially the Pauline letters, give more space to doctrine than to the place of baptism and Eucharist in the Church's life. Indeed, we know very little about how baptisms were performed or the Lord's Supper celebrated. But that they were performed and celebrated is obvious, as the casual introduction of references to them strikingly indicates. In Galatians 3, for example, baptism is introduced to explain what it means to be 'in Christ', and thus to be justified by faith. The argument shows what it means to be under the law, as a kind of discipline or imprisonment until the coming of Christ. But now that faith in Christ has come, we are no longer subject to a disciplinarian system:

> For in Christ Jesus you are all children of God through faith. As many of you as were baptised into Christ have clothed yourselves with Christ. There is no longer Jew or Greek, there is no longer slave or free, there is no longer male or female; for all of you are one in Christ Jesus.
>
> (Gal. 3:26–8, NRSV)

Professor Wayne Meeks has claimed that this way of speaking has its roots in certain aspects of the Adam

115

legends. For in these legends the 'image of God', which was lost when Adam sinned, was a garment of light. That image was both male and female, so the loss of it imposed a separation upon humankind. The clothing imagery 'interprets the ritual actions naturally associated with nude baptism'. The removal of clothing is a stripping away of the body of flesh (the 'spiritual circumcision' of Colossians 2:11); the baptism is a burial with Christ in the waters of death; reclothing afterwards is a putting on of Christ like a garment. 'The structural antinomies that establish one's social place, one's identity, are dissolved and replaced by a paradisaical unity: "All are one".' None of this needed explanation, apparently, to the Christian congregations of Galatia.[3]

A similar presupposition surrounds Paul's first introduction of a reference to the Lord's Supper. He is discussing the worship of idols, and the use of food sacrificed to idols. His purpose is to be sensitive to the difficulty of wholly escaping the ramifications of idolatry in a Gentile environment, while also taking into account Jewish scrupulousness. With regard to the latter, he advised careful separation: 'Have nothing to do with idolatry' (1 Cor. 10:14). And in this context, he reminds his readers that, 'When we bless the cup of blessing, is it not a means of sharing in the blood of Christ? When we break the bread, is it not a means of sharing in the body of Christ?' (1 Cor. 10:16). Here again there is the explication of intimacy 'in Christ', together with the implication of unity. A radical care for unity is also the context of a stunning denunciation of the gross divisions which arise at their meetings to eat the Lord's Supper – including a sharp instruction to 'discern the body' if they are to avoid falling under judgement, and so to observe the apparently elementary courtesy of waiting for each other at their meetings (1 Cor. 11:33f).

These examples are perhaps enough to demonstrate

that, for the communities to which the respective letters were written, the rituals of baptism and Eucharist were so familiar and secure of meaning as to be introduced as warrants in arguments of another kind. They tend to confirm the view of the social anthropologist that rituals take precedence over doctrines in the phenomenon of religion; that doctrines are, indeed, elaborations or explanations of the purposes and consequences of rituals. But before we go on to consider the implication of such a view for a Christian theology of sacrifice, we had better examine why 'ritualism' has become such a cause of anxiety to some strands of the Christian tradition.

MAGIC, RITUALS AND VAIN REPETITIONS

The basis for this anxiety emerges directly from the kind of definition given to ritual by anthropologists. For Meyer Fortes, for example, ritual is 'a procedure for prehending the occult'. This is explained as a threefold process: grasping what is occult in the events and incidence of peoples' lives, binding it by various techniques and beliefs, and incorporating it into people's normal daily lives. It is 'the executive arm' of a religious or magical system.[4] At once, the alarm-bells go off. The Christian faith has from the very first taken pains to distinguish itself from sorcery and magic (Acts 13:4–12, and 19:11–20). The occult, in popular language, carries a wholly negative connotation for the Christian. And the very idea that Christian rituals in some way constitute a technique for forcing God's arm directly contradicts at least one way of interpreting the freedom of God's grace.

There is, then, a serious difficulty in assimilating the anthropological vocabulary to the theological without careful criticism and commentary. Yet we notice that in the theologically acceptable category of 'the hidden', there

117

is a trace of one of the meanings of the term occult. God is a God who hides himself (Isa. 45:15). The gospel is God's hidden and secret wisdom (1 Cor. 2:7, Matt. 11:25). That is not to say that it is wholly concealed – but it is partly overt and partly hidden, at least to certain categories of people.

It is also important to note that at least one practising Roman Catholic anthropologist rather resists the theologian's instinct to distinguish sharply between the magical and the sacramental. In her classic work, *Natural Symbols*, Professor Mary Douglas insists on the defensibility of the idea of sacramental efficacy. The ritual works. But that is precisely the point of magic. She notes how a three-stage movement in and after the Reformation undermined confidence in ritual and symbolic forms: 'First, there is the contempt of external ritual forms; second, there is the private internalizing of religious experience; third, there is the move to humanist philanthropy. When the third stage is under way, the symbolic life of the spirit is finished.'[5] For the purpose of identifying what ritual means, she sees no advantage in distinguishing between the magical and the sacramental. 'The devotion of the sacraments ... depends on a frame of mind which values external forms and is ready to credit them with special efficacy'. It is not even completely satisfactory to distinguish sacramental efficacy, as working internally, from magical efficacy, as working externally:

> For if the theologian remembers to take account of the doctrine of the incarnation, magical enough in itself, and the even more magical doctrine of the Resurrection and of how power is channelled through the sacraments, he cannot make such a tidy distinction between sacramental and magical efficacy.[6]

Another way of making the same point would be to insist

on the bodiliness of the Christian religion, both of incarnation and resurrection, and to demonstrate the metaphorical character of the concept of 'interiority'. Something which works 'internally' does not work, for that reason, non-materially. There are physical brains to consider, as well as minds and souls. Faith has to do with brains as well as with souls. Words, ideas and images are physically processed as well as understood.

An essential part of the way in which rituals lodge themselves in human brains is by means of repetition. It will be objected that Jesus himself criticised the vain repetitions of those who 'imagine that the more they say the more likely they are to be heard' (Matt. 6:7). But he went on to deliver a prayer, the text of which has been more frequently repeated than any intercession in human history. Even so, some account must be made of the fact that Jesus received with approval the verse from Hosea 6:6, 'I desire mercy, not sacrifice' (Matt. 9:13; 12:7), and criticised the Pharisees for their ritual scrupulousness yet neglect of the greater matters of the divine law. Mary Douglas finds that she needs the concept of 'ritualised ritual' in order to speak of empty symbols of conformity, so as to preserve the possibility that observance of a ritual might signify a form of genuine conformity (p.21). In other words, the abuse of ritual must not be allowed to desensitise the believer to the importance of genuine ritual within a symbol-system.[7]

Consistent with this insight is a long-acknowledged prejudice in Protestant biblical criticism. Because Protestantism embraced a dogmatic anti-ritualism, the prophetic tradition of the Old Testament was depicted as standing on a higher level than the cultic or priestly tradition, out of which it was said to have developed or evolved. Whereas the prophetic tradition was ethical in character (so that account went), the priestly was magical and sub-ethical. Jesus himself stood firmly for the ethical values, but his religious genius was submerged by the recrudescence of magic and superstition in the patristic and medieval periods, to be liberated again at the Reformation. But even the Reformation was incomplete: only with the Enlightenment do we find a profounder grasp of the ethical substance of Jesus' teaching of the kingdom. This indeed has to be distinguished from some of the later theological ideas of Paul, who turned Christianity into an erudite doctrine of salvation. Such is the bare outline of an account of the belated rediscovery of the non-ritual character of original Christianity. In the light of this prejudice, documents were dated, sources detected and lined up in sequential developmental series, and whole strands of the tradition neglected or marginalised. That this grew from a dogmatic antipathy to ritual can scarcely be denied, even though its unmasking leaves us with the problem of ritualised ritual, a religious perversion detected by writers within the traditions of both Israelite religion and early Christianity.

A similar problem arises in the historical study of the Reformation, as Eamon Duffy's *The Stripping of the Altars* has so ably demonstrated.[8] There is a prejudice against 'superstitious rituals' which has informed the way in which the history of the English Reformation has been written. But the exposure of the cost and consequences of the loss of true rituals – channelling the devotion of many, and structuring society away from the domination of class or wealth – still leaves us with the problem of ritualised ritual, and of the criticism of magical rites which long predates the Reformation era. The question is whether there is a view of the sacraments which can respect the place of bodily rituals within Christian faith, without destroying the radicality of the demand for complete personal reorientation – the response of faith to God's justifying grace. At this point, we would do well to consider the question of sacrifice, which in the Old Testament is a class of ritual actions, but which in the New Testament is, as we have seen, one of the idea-complexes used to explain the death of Christ in the incipient theology of the atonement.

SACRIFICE AND SACRAMENT

It has already been shown in chapter 1 that the use of the word 'metaphor' in relation to the sacrifice of Christ presents some considerable complications. We have at least to take seriously that substantial part of the Christian tradition which considers the sacrifice of Christ to be definitive of what true sacrifice is. St Augustine wrote: 'The true sacrifice is offered in every act which is designed to unite us to God in a holy fellowship, every act, that is, which is directed to that final Good which makes possible our true felicity.'[9] The background to this definition is instructive, since Augustine is specifically concerned to distinguish true and false mediation between God and humanity. Christ alone offers us participation in his divine nature. To have holy fellowship with God means to have it through the sacrifice of the one and only mediator. Furthermore, by 'sacrifice' Augustine understands the duty owed by humanity to God, which is most adequately summed up by love of God and neighbour. He is at exceptional pains to describe the relationship between body and soul, exterior and interior, in the true worship of God. The strongest argument in favour of the centrality of sacrifice to atonement remains its intimate association with worship.[10]

There are complexities which need an explanation *en route* to such a theology. The Old Testament knows a large variety of ritual sacrifices, vegetable and animal. It also knows the metaphorical extension of the term 'sacrifice', sometimes called its spiritualisation, in such phrases as the 'sacrifice of thanksgiving' (Ps. 50:14; compare Pss. 27:6; 69:30; 107:22; 116:17), or the sacrifice of contrition (Ps. 51:17). George Herbert's remarkable poem, 'The Altar', which opens The Church (a section of his long poem 'The Temple') and whose text is shaped into the form of an altar, is both a visual representation of a church altar, and at the same time an evocation of the altar of the heart. It finishes:

> O let thy blessed SACRIFICE be mine,
> And sanctify this ALTAR to be thine.

As well as metaphorical extensions of sacrifice, the Old Testament insists on criteria by which ritualised ritual can be detected and discounted. These are conditions under which the due performance of sacrificial ritual is turned into a false, ineffectual or empty symbol. Among these conditions are: a wrong or inattentive disposition (Isa. 29:13) or gross injustice (Isa. 1:14–17). A striking sentence from the book of Proverbs combines them both:

> Sacrifice from a wicked person is an abomination to the Lord,
> the more so when it is offered from impure motives.
> (Prov. 21:27)

The early Christian communities inherited both the metaphorical extensions and the criteria for detecting ritualised ritual. Though there is no record of Jesus attacking the institution of ritual sacrifice, he is remembered as having quoted Hosea's warning, 'I require mercy, not sacrifice' (Hos. 6:6; cited in Matt. 9:13 and 12:13. Compare also Mark 12:33 referring to 1 Sam. 15:22). This is consistent with Jesus' demand for purity of intention as a condition of genuine repentance, and with his overt attack on the purity system and its underlying legislation.

Outside Jerusalem, synagogue Judaism was carrying on

its religious life to all intents and purposes without sacrifices. It was in this context that the tradition of Jesus' words at the Last Supper was handed on: how, when he took the cup, he had said, 'This is my blood, the blood of the covenant, shed for many' (Mark 14:24). The 'many' in the early Church were already celebrating the Eucharist each week, as a sacrificial meal of the risen Lord.[11] They believed that the old sacrificial system had been brought to an end by Jesus' death. The author of Hebrews ransacked the descriptions of Old Testament ritual in order to show how Christ's death had fulfilled it, and in fulfilling it brought it to a complete end.[12] What Christ's sacrifice had achieved was perfect forgiveness – and as a result, access to God. For St Paul, too, the death of Christ was the sacrificial, atoning death of the one who represented all humankind. We are therefore involved in it. We enter Christ's death and resurrection at baptism; we live his risen life through the Spirit of Christ. In a luminous phrase, St Paul implores his Roman congregation to offer themselves to God, 'a living sacrifice, dedicated and fit for his acceptance, the worship offered by mind and heart' (Rom. 12:1). These are the traditions, and it may be responsibly argued that Jesus himself saw his death as the sacrificial preparation for the coming of God's kingdom in the very face of the evil of its rejection.[13]

None the less there is formidable criticism to meet: that sacrifice is by no means central to the New Testament understanding of Christ's death; that it explains precisely nothing; that it has become progressively remote and unintelligible; that it has been abused by the ideologists of violence and warfare; that it exalts self-sacrifice in a way destructive to women in male-dominated societies.

That sacrifice has been abused as a concept – for example by Adolf Hitler – is beyond doubt. As a consequence the phrase 'sacrificial death' (*Opfer-tod*) is virtually unusable in German theology. Social Darwinism has had its influence throughout Western European culture, and in Nazi propaganda has been abused to justify the murder of the vulnerable in the supposed interests of the strong; their deaths, too, were classified as 'sacrificial'. It is also undeniable that self-effacing, even self-annihilating, behaviour has been recommended to women as supremely religious, and that popular ethics appear to demand that mothers (especially) sacrifice themselves for their children and husbands. These justified complaints incidentally demonstrate the continuing power of sacrifice, which is anything but a dead metaphor.

But sacrifice is far from being the only concept that is subject to misuse, even within the Church: 'power', for example (with which sacrifice is intimately connected), is another; 'freedom' was a source of considerable problems to St Paul; 'love' too has been subject to serious distortion. Were the opportunity of misuse a final reason for abandoning a concept, theology would consist of nothing but banalities. The answer to distortions is careful analysis. It is important to say, for example, that there is a distinction between deaths in wartime, and the sacrifice of Christ; that unreasonable demands are made of women, which should not be dignified with the epithet 'sacrificial'. Moreover, it is precisely because of the implications of Christ's sacrifice for the theme of power, as so often perceived by men (though not solely by men), that it is important to retain sacrifice in the theology of atonement.

At the same time, there is truth in the charge that sacrifice is not in any obvious sense an explanation of the effect of Christ's death.[14] When a social anthropologist speaks of 'the logic of sacrifice', he does not imply that there is a causal chain of events and consequences which every rational person could recognise as valid.[15] It is an exchange of some kind between God and humanity, involving the

giving of a gift. The gift (as all gifts) is relevant to, indeed
alters, the relationship. Christ's sacrifice is categorically
unique; if we did not make that claim for it, the term
'sacrifice' could easily be abandoned without loss.
Christ's sacrifice has three major and intended character-
istics: it constitutes an absolute commitment of body and
soul; it achieves the forgiveness of human sins; and it
represents a victorious conflict with the destructive negativity of power – a defeat of chaos and hatred by love. But
it is a mystery, and the insights we can achieve into how
the sacrifice of Christ 'works' are partial and elusive.

For many, sacrifice is most readily intelligible in relation
to commitment. Jesus' commitment to his vocation, his
doing of the will of his heavenly Father, his love for
his friends, and the connection he saw between the
kingdom and his suffering and death – these are the
aspects of his sacrifice for which we have some relevant
analogies in ordinary human experience. 'He gave himself
for us', is a way of expressing the sacrifice of absolute
commitment. Our lesser commitments are often ambiva-
lent – and mistaken commitments can be destructive. None
the less, nothing in human life is excepted in the offering
of our 'very selves' to God (Rom. 12:1). A prayer after
communion, in the 1662 Book of Common Prayer, put it
memorably:

> And here we offer and present unto thee, O Lord, ourselves,
> our souls and bodies, to be a reasonable, holy, and lively
> sacrifice unto thee ... And although we be unworthy,
> through our manifold sins, to offer unto thee any sacrifice,
> yet we beseech thee to accept this our bounden duty and
> service; not weighing our merits, but pardoning our
> offences, through Jesus Christ our Lord.

The verbal offering is to be followed by the practical, which
embraces the whole of life.

From this it follows that the sacraments of baptism and Eucharist – the major sacraments in all Christian sacramental traditions – are an initiation into, and a sustaining in, that life-offering. Baptism is, in fact, the contextualising of a human life within the narrative of Christ, a co-operative living of his life within the life of the Church, which is his body. One may properly speak of the baptismal sacrifice, in so far as it is an entry into the death and resurrection of Christ.[16] The new life of the baptised is described in a riotous variety of metaphors – of washing, rebirth, adoption, in-grafting, and so forth. But the substance of the rite is the claiming of the power of Christ's atoning death for entry upon the new life of the Spirit. At its most profound it is a declaration about the created powers of a living being as directed towards, and fulfilled in, mutual service, humility and love; it is thus an abandonment of the specious attractions of the world, the flesh and the devil.

The baptismal sacrifice is fundamental to the eucharistic, which is inseparable from it. Again, the reference is to the death and resurrection of Christ, who, as St Augustine insists, is both the priest making the offering and also the oblation. He continues: 'This is the reality, and he intended the daily sacrifice of the Church to be the sacramental symbol of this; for the Church, being the Body of which he is the head, learns to offer itself through him.'[17] There is, of course, a difference between Christ's sacrifice, and the sacrifice of members of the body of Christ. But the unity between them is the unity of fellowship with God, of holy communion, of the privilege of creaturely sharing in the divine life.

This understanding of sacrifice makes it central, not peripheral or optional, to the Christian faith. It has the effect of linking the sacramental rituals of both baptism and Eucharist to the story of Jesus, and thus to the theology of the atonement: baptism is a once-for-all immersion into Christ's death and resurrection; Eucharist is a repeated participation in the benefits of Christ's passion. Christ's own actions at the Last Supper interpret his death as the new covenant. The believer enters into a covenant of grace, which is God's own personal presence, by faith and baptism. These are distinguished, but not separable. The one is not internal and necessary, the other merely external and optional: both alike are bodily and spiritual, but in different measure. Baptism is initiation into the eucharistic community. Again, the two sacraments are distinguished, and only separable in an anomalous state of church disunity.

SACRAMENTS AND TIME

In the most obvious way, a baptism into Christ's death signifies a radical transaction with time. This is described by Professor Morna Hooker, in an impressive series of articles, as the 'pattern of exchange'.[18] We exchange our death for Christ's, and receive his life in place of our death. The logic of this transaction is, I believe, that of sacrifice, which draws the power of life from the giving away of life. This is not an exchange taking place merely in a transcendent realm. It is in our time that the Son of God dies, so that we may participate in his victory of death, and consequently live a resurrected life in our own time (Rom. 6:4).

But there is a still deeper context to this, in the election by God of his chosen people. The baptised are, after all, 'a chosen race, a royal priesthood, a holy nation' (1 Pet. 2:9). To receive the gift of baptism, therefore, is to enter an inheritance, whose praises so intoxicated the mind and overwhelmed the prose of the writer of the letter to the Ephesians (1:18). God chose us in Christ before the foun-

127

dation of the world to be holy and blameless before him in love. Because baptism is 'in Christ', the baptised participate in Christ's own election and mission.

If anything, the association of the Eucharist with God's time is even more obviously a feature of Christian teaching. Mysterious sayings of Jesus at the Last Supper link his covenantal death with the drinking of a new wine in God's kingdom. Eating the bread and drinking the cup are a proclamation of the death of Christ, 'until he comes' (1 Cor. 11:26). The Church's actions are pointers back to the events of the death and resurrection, and forward to the general resurrection and the events of the last times. The Church lives, therefore, out of both its memories and its hopes.

The most striking passage relating Eucharist and time is, however, John 6. A full discussion of why eating the flesh and drinking the blood of the Son is a eucharistic reference, and why it is not a late interpolation into the text, is beyond the scope of this book. But it is at least an obvious way to interpret the words, 'Whoever eats my flesh and drinks my blood has eternal life, and I will raise that person up on the last day' (John 6:54), as connecting eucharistic fellowship with participation in the benefits of Christ's death. It is also persuasive to interpret Johannine accounts of both baptism and Eucharist as expressing the way in which the believers publicly represent their adherence to the community of faith, and announce their separation from the outside world. There is a social and political significance to the community solidarity of those who are faithful to Jesus and to one another in love. Baptism marks the boundary and eucharistic fellowship reinforces it. These are public and social events, not private and individual.[19]

There are obvious differences between the way the other gospels speak of the kingdom, and the teaching of the

Fourth Gospel on 'eternal life'. But both to have eternal life and to be assured of resurrection 'on the last day' links present possession and future hope in a skilful synthesis. Nothing in John's gospel could encourage us to believe that we 'earn' eternal life – quite the contrary. It appears that we have eternal life the moment we receive the Word made flesh, and believe on his name (John 1:12). In that very moment, by a miracle of adoption, we become 'children of God', born 'from above' of water and Spirit (that is, I take it, both publicly in the water of baptism and secretly by the Spirit of God, John 3:5). Through this new birth a new life is possible, the life of mutual love (that of 'fellowship with one another'). Its secret content and substance is none other than fellowship with the Father and the Son, a privilege which follows as a consequence of the blood of Christ cleansing our sin (1 John 1:3–7). In different terminology, the substance is very similar. We have entered a new system, not of strict reciprocity, but of loving mutuality and of friendship. And this system is not ended by death. Indeed, the conquest of death's tyranny, its capacity to negate and render insignificant and even meaningless our spasmodic loves and feeble acts of generosity, is the heart of the Christian message. The question is: is it credible?

LIFE AFTER DEATH?

Belief in life after death is by no means secure, even among professed Christians. Various surveys have shown that, among church-going people, a not insignificant minority is doubtful about life after death. Life after death has also its theological critics, including those who say that it is unintelligible to speak of life being 'after' death, when the temporal sequence characteristic of life is simply halted at death for that person. He or she has no 'after'-life, as though the soul had jumped off one tired old horse to gallop into the sunset on another, as Feuerbach ridiculed the belief. Others again level moral criticism against belief in life after death as 'transcendental egoism', or as a subtle way of trying to avoid the moral claims which present injustice make on our conscience. A desire to survive death is said to be essentially selfish, and a distraction from the task of doing what we can to right the wrongs of the present social order.[20]

The root of these criticisms is the process called 'the moralisation of dogma', and it is similar to the process observed by Mary Douglas in relation to ritual. Indeed, one of the fiercest modern critics of the sacramental 'means of grace' was none other than the philosopher Immanuel Kant, who, at the end of his *Religion within the Limits of Reason Alone* (1793), sharply observed that trust in the causal efficacy of the sacraments was one of the excuses for not doing all one could to lead a good life. Scorning what he termed 'heathenish superstition', Kant interpreted baptism as a solemn beginning of a life of continuous moral education, and participation in the Eucharist as promoting the idea of a 'cosmopolitan moral community'. For Kant there can be no such thing as a supernaturally guaranteed knowledge of eternal life, though there is a 'practical' postulate of the immortality of the soul. Subsequent philosophical reflection has often tended to ignore the latter, and to focus on the moral implications of Christian doctrine. It is of this tradition that contemporary Christian scepticism about life after death is the unwitting heir. But in this scepticism, we are moving a step further on the road to reducing Christian faith to humanist philanthropy, as Mary Douglas observed. The question is, whether even the first step is a necessary one.

My suggestion is, in brief, that more is at stake in belief in the bodily resurrection than at first sight appears to be the case. The resurrection is, as we saw, not merely the ground of belief in justification, but also the fundamental element in a sacramental theology. It is undoubtedly a mysterious event, very difficult to construe with precision in the narratives we possess. The situation is not at all helped by those who defend the bodily resurrection as an essential ingredient of a more general fundamentalism. But it is utterly self-contradicting to refuse to accept that the scrutiny of evidence is relevant to a belief which has the truth of a historical proposition as its precondition. If the body of Jesus was said to be in the tomb at one time, and later was not in the same tomb, then it is relevant to know upon what evidence that assertion is based. The lack of uniformity between the accounts of the event, which the biblical historian is bound to notice, tells in favour of their authenticity and general reliability, rather than the reverse.[21] The utter mysteriousness of what occurred is enhanced, not diminished, by acknowledging elements of mythology in some of the later narratives.

The defence of the bodily resurrection which commends itself to me is one which believes that *our* bodiliness is involved in testifying to the power of the living Christ. We are always carrying about in our bodies the death of Jesus, said St Paul, with reference to his various ordeals, 'so that the life of Jesus may also be made visible in our bodies' (2 Cor. 4:10). The ascension of Jesus is followed by the bodiliness of our witness. Where did Jesus' body go? That is a peculiar question, based on ignoring the extraordinary quality of Jesus' risen body in the narratives of his appearances. Could one have photographed the risen Jesus? It is a question not capable of a straight answer. Jesus was real to Thomas. Whether he would be felt in the same way by all, we do not know. Why should we know more than the narratives? It may be that, in Jesus' resurrection appearances, God granted to the first disciples enough assurance to enable them to be certain that Jesus was victorious in his struggle with death, and confidently to live the next episode of the story of the triumph of grace. With the help of the Holy Spirit, the disciples themselves become the main evidence for the resurrection. This evidence is also embodied, and the matter which sustains the evidence is physical likewise, in water and bread and wine.

There are many who cannot 'hear' the story of the resurrection, for whom grief or torment or deprivation or incapacity have proved too strong. In relation to them, the Christian is not helpless, because the resurrection is not a 'conjuring trick with words', but a pattern of life towards, a being with, an action on behalf of, others. Resurrection can be, and should be, embodied in liberative social actions, in hugs for the vulnerable, and energetic research into the cure of disease and the mitigation of disability.

That kind of life is sustained by the sacraments, which are an integral part of the rich symbolic life of the spirit. Sacraments, we saw, contain both memory and hope; they look back and forward; they contextualise and inform the present. They set us out of our time, the more securely to root us in our time. They remind us of the sacrifice of Christ, so as both to energise and to humble our own efforts at self-oblation. They inspire both sobriety and joy. They are distinguishable from faith, but inseparable from it. They are simple actions, but are also deeply mysterious. They remind us of our bodiliness, but they liberate us from the body of death. They help us put on the unfamiliar garment of imperishability, and give us the confidence to work without ceasing, steadfastly for the Lord.

6

ooooooooo

A theology of evangelism

Evangelism has a wretched public reputation. We can trace this in the first instance to the rise, decline and fall of certain notorious media evangelists caught in financial or (occasionally and) sexual misdemeanours. It was an eerie experience to be reading Sinclair Lewis's masterly portrait of a delinquent evangelist in *Elmer Gantry* (1927), and to be hearing at the same time of the unmasking of a contemporary American practitioner of his arts. But even if we set on one side the grosser displays of greed and self-deception (which is easier to do in Europe where they have less of an impact), there is still a problem about evangelism, indeed about evangelicalism as a whole. It is a problem specific to a particular type of piety within Christianity, which does not cling to the same degree to the piety of Catholicism. In my view, it is connected to the nineteenth-century Evangelical critique of 'worldliness', and to the conscious formulation of the profile of a 'real Christian' – a personage with all the attractions of a culturally philistine, censorious and narrow-minded bigot.

There is a brilliant exploration of this theme in Karen Blixen's short story 'Babette's Feast', made into an exceptional film of the same name.[1] It concerns the holding of a gourmet feast in the context of a narrow, pietistic Lutheran community of mid-nineteenth century Scandinavia. The event is planned and realised by a French Catholic *emigrée*, Babette – a cook of international renown. The villagers,

133

despite their initial misgivings, come to enjoy the excellent food and wine, and their pious hymns and aspirations, grown sour with the restrictedness of their personal and social lives, take on renewed inspiration. At a showing of the film to a somewhat sophisticated audience, I became conscious of the audience's desire to mock the narrow-mindedness of the pietistic group. The film's reticence in this regard was unusual and notable, and the gradual transformation of the pietistic community, by means of the act of feasting, was portrayed with sensitivity. Without unduly forcing the theme, it was possible to see a eucharistic meaning in the combination of Evangelical piety and Catholic worldliness.

But negativity in relation to the created world is a serious charge to bring against a major tradition of Christian discipleship. It is also partly unfair. Like the accusatory use of the term 'puritan', it displays a certain selective blindness to the evidence of pre-Reformation intolerance and narrowness. Negativity – as regards sexuality, for example – is as much a feature of standard Catholicism as it ever was in the Protestant denominations. But there is still a serious case to answer on the subject of Evangelical rejection of 'worldliness', which was frequently taken to include ordinary enjoyment of the cultural opportunities of the created order. The fact that so many artists lived 'non-Christian lives' was taken by Evangelicals to imply that one heard, read or viewed their works with distant suspicion. It is as if the totality of the world were so engulfed by the event of conversion, that everything that does not contribute directly to it, or lead directly from it, is liable to be regarded as a distraction or temptation.

Evangelicals have suffered from this reputation. There are literary portrayals – for example in Samuel Butler's The *Way of All Flesh* (1903) – where this is brought out. For example, 'Sims' or Simeonites – followers of the Evangelical Anglican preacher, Charles Simeon (1759–1836) of Cambridge – were thought not to wash too frequently, to be boorish and to have designs upon people's enjoyments and allegiances. And part of that reputation is justified and perhaps unavoidable. The Gospel contains a critical edge; and no one likes to be thought to be morally in the wrong. But evangelism also suffers from the perception that it is based in a censorious and narrow view of life. It is culturally unpopular, and it seems to sustain itself by opting out of culture, and by creating a total environment, a narrow fellowship in which reassurance come from, everyone being of the same mind. How much of this unpopularity is simply inevitable, and how much is rooted in theological mistakes? That is the question for this chapter.

EARLY EVANGELISM

When we turn to the earliest documents of the New Testament, we can see clearly enough that both criticism of the surrounding culture and an answering hostility was part of the situation. St Paul's first letter to the Thessalonians is, in all probability, the first complete document giving evidence for the existence and life of the Christian Church. The standard view is that it was written in about AD 50, a year after Paul had founded a congregation in Thessalonica, on a visit from Philippi. The greeting to the church is 'from Paul, Silvanus [called Silas in Acts] and Timothy' (1:1); they had brought the Gospel earlier (v.5), and the success of the message had ramifications for other areas in Macedonia and Achaea. Chapter 2 of the letter gives a tantalising glimpse of how the mission had been conducted and the controversy it had aroused. Chapter 3 indicates that there had been a follow-up visit by Timothy from Athens, to encourage the new converts in the face of 'hardship' Acts 17:1–10 specifically mentions a riot brought about by disaffected Jews, following Paul's exposition of the biblical support for the claim that Jesus is Messiah:

> Following his usual practice Paul went to their meetings; and for the next three sabbaths he argued with them, quoting texts of scripture which he expounded and applied to show that the Messiah had to suffer and rise from the dead. 'And this Jesus', he said, 'whom I am proclaiming to you is the Messiah.' Some of them were convinced and joined Paul and Silas, as did a great number of godfearing Gentiles and a good many influential women. (Acts 17:2–4)

On this showing, Christianity is undeniably a religion of conviction open to Jews and Gentiles, men and women, slaves and the influential. It makes specific claims about Jesus, which throughout history some have believed and others have doubted. These claims Paul refers to as 'the Gospel' (*euangelion*): 'When we brought you the gospel we did not bring it in mere words [*logos*] but in the power of the Holy Spirit and with strong conviction' (1 Thess.1:5; see also 1 Cor. 2:4). Conviction is a word also used in Colossians 2:2 ('My aim is to keep them in good heart and united in love, so that they may come to the full wealth of conviction which understanding brings, and grasp God's secret, which is Christ himself'), and in Hebrews 6:11 ('We want each one of you to show the same diligence, so as to realise the full assurance of hope to the very end', NRSV).

The passionate quality of that term is mirrored in Paul's account of his own integrity and personal commitment. In preaching this Gospel there is no indulgence of delusions, no hint of financial motives, no deception, no flattery, no self-magnification. There is reticence, even, about the divine origins of the message, and the divine commission of the messenger. Paul betrays sensitive awareness of the ambivalence of the power-claim entailed in being 'Christ's envoy':

> Although as Christ's own envoys we might have made our
> weight felt; but we were as gentle with you as a nurse caring
> for her children. Our affection was so deep that we were
> determined to share with you not only the gospel of God
> but our very selves; that is how dear you had become to us!
> (1 Thess.2:7f)

All this contrasts starkly with the hostility he and his
young converts had encountered at the hands of local
Jews. Persecution is, Paul explains, a common fate which
also befell Christians in Judaea. But Jews were responsible
for the death of Jesus, and 'are so heedless of God's will
and such enemies of their fellow-men that they hinder us
from telling the Gentiles how they may be saved' (1 Thess.
2:15–16). Hard words follow. The Jews have been 'making
up the full measure of their guilt'. But now 'retribution'
(*orge*) has overtaken them. We remember that Paul himself
was a Jew – nor is it clear to what he is referring by
'retribution' or 'wrath'. But his correspondents would be
in no doubt that the message of salvation entailed deliver-
ance from retribution. 'The day of the Lord' is about to
break upon them, and so they must be alert and watchful,
'armed with the breastplate of faith and love, and the hope
of salvation for a helmet' (1 Thess. 5:2, 8). 'God has not
destined us for retribution [*orge*], but for the full attain-
ment of salvation through our Lord Jesus Christ. He died
for us so that awake or asleep we might live in company
with him' (1 Thess.5:9–10). Again, Christianity is undeniably a religion of conviction, whose fruit is salvation. It
involves a 'transfer of loyalty and a sense of belonging
from one set of social relations to another, quite different
set'. Christians have acquired a new reference-group, and
their experience was set 'within an explanatory narrative
with broad metaphorical power and extended behavioural
implications'.[2] The Christian's task is to share the Gospel

of God in such a way that all people move from darkness to light, from the threat of retribution to the full enjoyment of salvation.

A theology of evangelism is based in an understanding of salvation – specifically, of atonement. The noun 'evangelism' appears later in English than the verb 'to evangelise'. This is not surprising: there is no Greek noun corresponding to the English 'evangelism', defined as 'the preaching or promulgation of the Gospel, the performance of the work of an evangelist'. There is real advantage in preserving the active verbal form, 'to evangelise', which enters English through Wycliffe's translations of the Old and New Testament (1380). It is striking, for example, that he translates the familiar, 'thou that tellest good tidings to Zion', as 'thou that evangelisest to Sion' (Isa. 40:9).

It has been argued in this book that narrative or story is fundamental to understanding salvation, and more particularly atonement. The story of salvation provides the overarching interpretative context in which the Christian lives his or her life. The reality of salvation is the delivery from retribution or wrath, the removal from the realm of darkness to that of light, participation in the resurrection of Jesus Christ from the dead, justification by grace, received by faith. That transition, however gradual it may be in experience, is given a focal point in time in the physical ritual of baptism. But baptism has continually to be received in a daily turning from sin and rising to newness of life, and there plainly are degrees of participation in that reality.

The theology of evangelism (or better, of evangelising) has to do on the one hand with the way 'Gospel' (*euangelion*) is understood, and on the other with the implications of that understanding for the Christian's approach to sharing his or her convictions. The first task we have already carried out in large measure in previous chapters.

There remains, however, one considerable problem which has to do with the 'retribution' of which Paul speaks, and which is also contained in the biblical symbol of hell, because it affects both the motives and manner of evangelising. To put it bluntly, does the desire to save people from hell and damnation constitute the main reason for evangelising? To this issue we must now turn.

JUDGEMENT AND CONDEMNATION

It has recently been argued, persuasively, both that judgement has been neglected in Christian theology of late, and that it needs to be firmly and clearly restored as a structural part of the doctrines essential to Christian identity.[3] We have already seen in chapter four that the implication of Christ's resurrection is that all human beings will rise from death and will be judged by the one who 'stands ready to judge the living and the dead' (1 Pet. 4:5). This is not the same as the doctrine of the natural immortality of the soul, which has a more metaphysical character. A resurrection to judgement, in virtue of Christ's resurrection from the dead, has a narrative quality about it. It is the continuation of the story of my life 'after' my death. When I die, I, together with everyone else, will be held accountable to God for what I have done.

This judgement is an essential part of unravelling the ambiguity by which I am at present surrounded, and my inveterate failure even to understand myself and my own motives. At present we do not enjoy perfect sight or insight: 'My knowledge now is partial; then it will be whole, like God's knowledge of me' (1 Cor.13:12). The implications of 'then' are explored by St Paul in chapter 15, on the resurrection of the dead. But the point is unmistakable. There is to be an unravelling of the perplexities in which we are caught. There is to be a perfecting of the limited knowledge which we have now of God and of his will.

Boldly, the author of 1 John expresses his hope in the following way:

> Dear friends, we are now God's children; what we shall be has not yet been disclosed, but we know that when Christ appears we shall be like him, because we shall see him as he is. As he is pure, everyone who has grasped this hope makes himself pure. (1 John 3:2–3)

The implication of this fact of being held accountable, together with the hope of being put right, places the believer in a situation of some understandable anxiety. Again, Paul expresses it with clarity in a passage (in 1 Corinthians) of reflection on his own performance as a preacher of the Gospel. He has had to negotiate major ambiguities in his relationship with Jews and with Gentiles. This has required considerable self-discipline, which he administers to himself like a boxer or athlete: 'I do not spare my body, but bring it under strict control, for fear that after preaching to others I should find myself disqualified' (1 Cor. 9:27). The possibility of a fall from grace into worthlessness and rejection is real, and a cause of vigilance. In 1 Peter the Christian is exhorted to be alert and on guard: 'Your enemy the devil, like a roaring lion, prowls around looking for someone to devour' (1 Pet. 5:8). We have already examined the tradition which speaks of graduated reward within the context of justification. It appears that part of this projected narrative of future accountability is the common-sense possibility that feeble efforts of discipleship will be rewarded less generously than whole-hearted commitment: 'For we must all have our lives laid open before the tribunal of Christ, where each must receive what is due to him for his conduct in the body, good or bad' (2 Cor.5:10).

There is, then, a future judgement, and the believer has to take seriously the possibility of condemnation and punishment. Do not the same considerations apply to the non-believer? To be sure, we have argued that it is impossible to hold that all who have lived out of contact with historic revelation and the life of the Church are, for that reason alone, debarred from salvation. But that does not necessarily imply the salvation of all. And there are blunt statements throughout the New Testament to the effect that human beings face the starkest of choices between darkness and light, between death and life. We may cite merely one such passage, 1 John 5:11–12: 'God gave us eternal life, and this life is in his Son. Whoever has the Son has life; whoever does not have the Son of God does not have life' (NRSV). Is this teaching an integral part of a theology of evangelising? Is it not bound to constitute its prime motive?

We should first identify and then correlate the two traditions which have arisen from this question. The first of these is the unmistakable element of threat – indeed of fear – which is present also in the recorded preaching of Jesus. The disciple is specifically told to fear the one who is able to destroy the soul and body in hell (Gehenna, the name for the place of fiery torment reserved for the wicked, Matthew 10:28); if one has a wandering and adulterous eye it would be better to tear it out than for the whole body to be cast into hell (Matt. 5:30); the vipers' brood of Scribes and Pharisees are fit only for condemnation to hell (Matt 23:15 and 33); a parable of Jesus places the rich man (who had ignored Lazarus the poor man) after his death in Hades (the abode of the dead), and in fiery torment (Luke 16:19–31). Not merely do these vivid statements and illustrations imply a state of acute danger for one who is attempting to make an appropriate response

141

to God's will, but Jesus also states that there will not be many who do so:

> Enter by the narrow gate. Wide is the gate and broad the road that leads to destruction and many enter that way; narrow is the gate and constricted the road that leads to life and those who find them are few. (Matt. 7:13–14)

This note of anxiety about the tendency and drift of human culture is also present in the Pauline letters and the Johannine literature. In the latter it is summed up in one of the uses of the term 'the world'. 'We know', says the writer of 1 John, 'that we are of God's family, but that the whole world lies in the power of the evil one' (1 John 5:19).

But there is a second tradition to note, which is present also in the Gospel of John, and is represented in Jesus' conversation with Nicodemus:

> God so loved the world that he gave his only Son, that everyone who has faith in him may not perish but have eternal life. It was not to judge the world that God sent his Son into the world, but that through him the world may be saved (John 3:16–17).

Comment on the theme of judgement is also present in Matthew's Sermon on the Mount: 'Do not judge, and you will not be judged' (Matt. 7:1). It is required of disciples that they observe their own faults before remarking on those of others. This is consistent with the striking theme of generosity of treatment in the matter of sin, contained in the vivid parable of the unmerciful debtor (Matt. 18:23–35), and in the maxim, redolent of the wisdom tradition, that you should always treat others in the way you want to be treated your self (Matt. 7:12).

There is, moreover, a remarkable passage in 1 John which contains a commentary precisely on the relationships of judgement, fear and love – and which may be a commentary on the passage (John 3:16–17) cited above.[4] This whole section (1 John 4:6b–21) concerns the love which ought to exist between friends within the Christian community. It is based on faith that Jesus is God's Son, as a result of which we know that his death is the utmost revelation of God's love for humanity, the sins of humanity are forgiven, and God dwells in love in the believer. This love breeds confidence in the face of judgement (see also 1 John 2:28; 2:21). What he has written about final judgement was not intended to breed fear in the believer's heart and mind: 'In love there is no room for fear; indeed perfect love banishes fear. For fear has to do with punishment, and anyone who is afraid has not attained to love in its perfection' (1 John 4:18). The love which exits, or should exist, between fellow-Christians is a sign that they participate in God's own life, and therefore share his life.

There is need for considerable further reflection on the implications of this passage. The whole purpose of the letter is perhaps to sharpen the boundaries between two Christian groups, one of which, from the author's perspective, has seceded and become Antichrist (1 John 2:18–19). It appears that the love which is commended stops sharply at the boundary separating them. It is anything but universal benevolence. Because the secessionists have embraced the spirit of error and followed false prophets, it is simply stated that they do not participate in God's love. Yet the author of the letter is no simple sectarian, anxious to reinforce his own plausibility structures against a hostile world. The Johannine love-ethic may be seen as an interpretation and intensification of Jesus' command to love our enemies, explicitly based on the love of God for all, even the unrighteous (Luke 6:35–6).[5]

What the Fourth Gospel creates by this interpretation is a radical version of the social implications of the Gospel.

To be saved is not simply to enjoy the individual blessing of the forgiveness of sin and hope of eternal life; it is necessarily and inescapably also to participate in a community of love. If being in such a community attracts persecution and dissent, the escape-route is not a form of private reassurance. It comes from an intensification of the experience of mutual love, held as it were proleptically, on behalf of all humanity. It is the whole world which God loves, its hostility and wickedness notwithstanding. The Christian community does not withdraw from contact with the world, in order to celebrate the salvation of the few within the walls of a holy ghetto. It stands for, and represents, the love of God for all people, in spite of its being misunderstood. Though it becomes exclusive because of the negative reaction of the world, its fundamental principle and instinct is that of open love and generosity.

There are, then, two rather different traditions concerning the motive for evangelism. Both of them have played a substantial role in the history of Christian missionary endeavour. On the one hand it is clear that threat and anxiety about future judgement has motivated foreign missions. There are stories of anxious converts asking why a loving God did not bring the missionaries earlier to their country to save their parents.[6] There were also active missionaries who vigorously dissented. Yet there is more to depicting a situation of acute danger than the fear of hell. The vivid picture of someone preferring to tear out an eye, or cut off a hand, casts light on the urgency of what is at stake in temptation. The rich man's presence in torment, for no other reason (apparently) than the fact that he was rich during his lifetime, dramatically reinforces Jesus' warning about the dangers of wealth. We may revolt from a theology which depicts God as damning all who live or have lived beyond sight and sound of the Gospel

144

– but the alternative is not to drift into indifference or complacency.

The second tradition comes to memorable expression in a hymn sometimes attributed to St Francis Xavier, 'O Deus ego amo Te, Nec amo Te ut salves me', and translated by the Roman Catholic convert, Edward Caswell, for his *Lyra Catholica* of 1849:

> My God, I love thee, not because
> I hope for heaven thereby,
> Nor yet because who love thee not
> Are lost eternally.

Recalling the passion, the hymn continues:

> Why then, O blessed Jesu Christ,
> Should I not love thee well?
> Not for the sake of winning heaven,
> Nor of escaping hell.
>
> Not for the hope of gaining aught,
> Not seeking a reward;
> But as thyself has loved me
> O ever-loving Lord.

This is an authentic expression of that perfect love which banishes fear, and is lived in for its own sake. Rabia, a ninth-century Sufi mystic, writes in similar vein:

> O God! if I worship Thee in fear of Hell, burn me in Hell; and if I worship Thee in hope of Paradise, exclude me from Paradise; but if I worship Thee for Thine own sake, withhold not Thine Everlasting Beauty![7]

Again, we may comment that there is no necessary contradiction between regarding the human situation as urgent, and yet at the same time putting aside a pressing anxiety about final salvation as the motivation for evangelising.

The conventional attribution of the poem (quoted above) to St Francis Xavier shows at least an awareness that missionary endeavour is not impossible for those whose main motivation is not ideas of reward and punishment.

How can this come about? The answer appears to lie in the curious capacity of narrative, as the raw material of theology, to inform the mind in rather different ways. We have already observed the fact that the strict translation of the narrative of salvation into theology makes Trinitarian theology impossible. A Miltonian epic, memorable and attractive though it appears at first sight, cannot make sense of the relationship of Father and Son, as Trinitarian theology requires. Some narrative of God sending his Son is, however, absolutely indispensable. No substitute for this narrative achieves the same effect or would have the same authority. There is no alternative but to suspend in the mind the implications of literalism – we do not imagine to ourselves a scene in heaven in which the Father and the Son converse with each other about how humanity is going to be saved. But both strands of the narrative are necessary. The Father sends the Son; the Son offers himself to the Father. Though literally incapable of being combined in a single narrative, they inform the mind in different ways.

We can see something similar taking place in relation to judgement and condemnation. The narrative of salvation requires an event at which human beings are held accountable for their lives and are judged. This accountability is extremely serious. Those who misuse their God-given powers are in danger of condemnation, and of punishment in unquenchable fire. None the less the character of the judge is one of love – our judge commands us to love even our enemies and persecutors. This judge himself was condemned – and still he loves his creation and his creatures. Those who live in his love find themselves moved beyond fear of punishment; simply to be motivated by fear contradicts the quality of the relationship into which they have entered. Both narratives are required – though they are, strictly speaking, incompatible. But at a crucial, and perhaps unknown, level in the mind, the literal consequences of holding both are refused and the traditions are sustained together to inform attitudes in different ways. When focusing on the potential of the human heart for radical wickedness, nothing is too strong by way of warning. When focusing on the gracious invitation of the love of God, both our hope of reward and fear of punishment fall into the background.

HELL AND UNIVERSALISM

We do not, however, so easily dispense with the highly charged arguments about the eternity of the punishments of hell, into which F.D. Maurice entered in his controversial work, *Theological Essays* (1853), which led to his resignation from a theological chair at King's College, London. Nor do we need so distant an example. Writing in *The Spectator* in 1992, the then British Minister of education, John Patten, a Roman Catholic, articulated the feared social consequences of loss of belief in redemption and damnation:

> It has a profound effect on personal morality – especially on criminality. It is, to me, self-evident that we are born with a sense of good and evil. It is also self-evident that as we grow up each individual chooses whether to be good or bad. Fear of eternal damnation was a message reinforced through attendance at church every week. The loss of that fear has meant a critical motive has been lost to young people when they decide whether to try to be good citizens or to be criminals.[8]

147

In the 1850s it was fear of the loss of belief in the eternity of punishment which alarmed the Church. But so suspicious have theologians become of the connection between fear of eternal punishment and social control of the 'underclass', that John Patten's adventure into theological enquiry was largely ignored or criticised as simplistic.

The connection between theology and social thought can be given further illustration. It has been observed that there is a substantial connection between the revulsion against certain penal practices in England in the early nineteenth century and changes in atonement theory. Moral criticism of the Protestant theory of the atonement, which spoke of Christ's death as penal satisfaction for the sins of humanity, can be dated with some precision to 1831, and the controversial views of a young Scotsman, John McLeod Campbell (1800–72). The main point of his work on the atonement (published in 1856, after his conviction for heresy and deprivation in 1831) was that Christ made perfect intercession for human sin, but not that he was punished for that sin.[9] Fifteen years earlier, five men had been put to death, convicted of theft and damage to property in Littleport, near Ely, and sixteen others had been deported. A tablet recording that fact as a warning was placed (and is still visible) on an outside wall of St Mary's Church in Ely. But the draconian punishment was widely regarded as intolerable, and public criticism mounted.

With the growth of understanding about the unconscious desires and motivations of human beings, grossly punitive solutions to the problem of sin began to appear morally crude and psychologically naïve. In the twentieth century, the theory of punishment for crime took a strongly rehabilitative turn, and the spotlight was turned on environmental influences and upbringing. Alternatively, in response to a more mechanistic model of human behaviour, and to changes in moral theory which denied objectivity to good and evil, socially undesirable actions were held to be capable of 'treatment' by various forms of manipulation, including drug regimes designed to build up aversion, administered along with rewards for conformity. The current levels of crime – eloquent testimony to the failure to 'cure' criminal behaviour – have put penal theory into crisis, and the most recent fashion is again for straightforward retributive punishment, barely constrained by the profession of adherence to humane standards.

There is no obvious reason why Christian theology should trudge earnestly in the footsteps of fashion in penal theory. It is, however, intelligible why it may tend to do so. The theological tradition of the Old Testament emphasised that God is just – the establishment of God's rule in Israel involved obedience to a highly detailed code of behaviour, both social and ritual. At the same time, sophisticated evasions of the primary requirements of such observance were (as we have seen) sharply criticised by the prophets in the name of a more generalised understanding of what is just. The implication of the New Testament is that the ritual codes have been abandoned. God's justice is understood in the more generalised sense, though given a greater theological and personal content in justification by grace. The social implications of God's justice remain relatively undeveloped. Law-making in human societies – embodying an understanding of the degree to which human beings should be liable to be punished retributively for their offences – has varied widely, even in societies influenced by Christian teaching. Justice is expressed in detailed, 'thick' codes, completely interwoven with the values and norms of a particular society at a particular time.[10] There might well be argument about this or that feature: only participants in a particular context, familiar

149

with its traditions, would recognise the force of those arguments. In time, internal criticism might lead to changes.

A Christian understanding of social justice is not of one single 'thick' tradition. Changes occur in the way in which the detailed implications of God's justice are understood – and these changes have consequences for developed theories of atonement. Theological justice is a *'thin'* account of God's dealings with humankind. It is expressed in general principles, not in elaborate and detailed particulars. We can be assured that he does not behave capriciously, that he has no favourites. His good is not evil; his love is not hate. And we know that he is a merciful judge; in that sense God can be expected to have insight into what we would now call 'mitigating circumstances'. It is intelligible how the tradition of severity which we have considered might come to be differently construed in the light of developments in the 'thick' codes of particular penal theories. Yet it remains vital that we see wrongdoing for what it is, and confront it in ourselves and in others with honesty and courage.

But does God send people to hell for eternity? That was the blunt issue, to which F.D. Maurice responded negatively on moral grounds, providing various kinds of exegetical escape from terms such as 'eternal' in certain biblical passages. He was consequently accused of being a universalist – that is, of holding the doctrine that ultimately all people will be saved. More recent universalists have proposed that God's love is to be seen on the analogy of an infinitely wise psychologist with an infinite amount of time to spend, capable of unravelling the tightest of knots of resistance and hostility. It is argued that to set a limit to this love is theologically untenable, tantamount to denying God's omnipotence and resulting in a dualism of eternal good and evil co-existing without reconciliation. How do we respond to this?

We have already seen that the Christian can have no moral or theological interest in *insisting* that God punishes for all eternity large numbers of people who live (and lived) outside the range of his explicit covenants. On the contrary: there is every reason to hope that, just as God's dealings with me are characterised by grace, so too he graciously embraces those who do not profess the faith. But that is not to condone indifference or complacency. Many pastors are asked by anxious relatives whether their deceased kith and kin 'will be all right'. The question has to be answered with both grace and integrity. The judgement is in God's hands. It will not do to imply that God is simply indulgent of sin. He does not treat sin as though it were not sin – that would not be moral, as Anselm observed. If the pastor is not called on to condemn the deceased for failure to profess the Christian faith in word and deed, neither is he or she to misrepresent the present situation and demand. The truth that Christ died for the sins of all is the only basis for prayers either of commendation or for the soul of the departed; and such prayer, by implication, is a reminder of the seriousness of sin.

The substitution of amiability for the demands of costly love in the modern Church is a reflection of the same substitution in the doctrine of God. The crucial issue in the doctrine of universalism is not whether God's love is ultimately irresistible (which we cannot know), but whether our conception of God's love is of holy love, a burning fire of love which purges the complacency of our mere amiability. The challenge of Johannine spirituality is of a brotherhood and sisterhood of sacrificial generosity. In such a context, we may lose our fear of hell without suffering undue harm. In most modern Christian communities, characterised by the acutest difficulties in sustaining the ordinary virtue of forgiveness, it would be

safer to remember the dénouement to Matthew's version
of the parable of the unmerciful debtor:

> So angry was the master [with his behaviour] that he con-
> demned the man to be tortured until he should pay the
> debt in full. That is how my heavenly Father will deal with
> you, unless you each forgive your brother from your hearts.
>
> (Matt 18:34–5)

PRAISE: A MOTIVE FOR EVANGELISM

In a certain sense, our discussion of evangelism has so far
proved inconclusive. We have noted the negative cultural
image which has dogged both evangelism and evangelicalism since the nineteenth century. At the same time,
one of the traditions of the New Testament contains an
unmistakeable note of critical urgency, directed as much
at the believer as the unbeliever. It is the Christian disciple
in danger of lapsing into indifference or heresy who is so
seriously warned – much as Jesus' address to his fellow
Jews contains an overt element of rebuke and judgement.
At the same time, we also noted a significant strand of
teaching which has put fear behind it, in speaking of the
love of God. But neither tradition seems to provide a
comprehensive context and motive for evangelism, capable
of including both emphases and of meeting the charge of
philistinism.

The proposal I wish to make is that the praise of God,
in word and deed, should be the leading context and
motive for evangelising. The urgency of evangelism stems
from Christians longing to share the sense of gratitude
which overwhelms them, in the light of God's gracious
gift of himself. They should make no distinction between
insiders and outsiders, between, as it were, the probably
saved and the possibly damned. It is not a question of

targeting this or that group or individual in order to achieve their conversion. In that way, what is inevitably communicated is anxiety and a certain desire to dominate. Instead, it is as if Christians were extending an invitation to join a choir to someone known to have a good voice – so that a particular contribution can be made in the chorus of praise of God's glory. The invitation is extended to all, whether they present themselves as inside or outside. It is based on gratitude for what God has already done, and a longing that God's praises will grow.

Both of the traditions we have mentioned can be included in this context. Undeniably, human beings can make a disastrous mess of their lives. A great deal is at stake for individuals and whole communities in wilfully defiling God's creation and abusing its powers. But the desire to escape the destructiveness of which human beings are capable does not provide a sufficient motive for evangelising. That has to be positive, because it alone provides the authentic tone or note of gratitude for God's superfluous generosity in all his gifts. So the motive of praise embraces the other tradition too, which emphasises the love of God for his own sake – a love which puts fear behind it and grows through the praise of the beloved.

Among God's gifts are those of the powers and beauty of creation. No praise of God which excludes the song of the valleys thick with corn could possibly be adequate to the gifts of God (Ps. 65). To make the praise of God the motive of evangelising thus addresses the potential narrowness of those who focus exclusively on the event of conversion. A Trinitarian approach to evangelising has a capacity to interlink the created order, the gift of redemption through the death of Christ, and the life of the Spirit-filled community, the Church. These are not to be seen as competitive focuses of attention, any more than joy at the beauty of creation is to be gained at the expense of anguish and anger at the injustice of so much catastrophic and avoidable deprivation.[11] God's 'saving power' among the nations unites his judgement of the people in righteousness, with the praises of the people at harvest (Ps. 67).

A passage from St Paul's second letter to the Corinthians explicitly suggests the comprehensiveness of the task of praise (2 Cor. 4:13–5). It is significantly set in the context of an argument concerning the character of Paul's commission as an apostle. He calls it a 'ministry of the Spirit' (2 Cor. 3:8) because it mediates a new, spiritual covenant more glorious than the old covenant of Sinai. That is what his apostleship is about – the open declaration of God's truth in Jesus Christ, an unveiling of his glory. God, he says, 'has caused his light to shine in our hearts, the light which is the knowledge of the glory of God in the face of Jesus Christ' (2 Cor. 4:6).

This glory contrasts sharply with the fate of his own body under persecution. Despite this, he carries the death of Jesus around with him precisely so that the risen life of Jesus can also be made clear in his body. It is faith in the resurrection which makes all the difference. Out of that faith comes the ministry of proclamation. The one who raised Jesus from the dead will also raise Paul, and his correspondents with him. Everything of which he has spoken – God's call to him, his ministry, his suffering – all is for their sake, 'so that, as the abounding grace of God is shared by more and more, the greater may be the chorus of thanksgiving that rises to the glory of God' (2 Cor. 4:15). This is what gives him continuing confidence, despite all the difficulties.

Two further reflections should give us some assurance that joining the praise of God has the capacity to motivate Christian evangelising. The first concerns the importance of the kingdom of God in Jesus' own teaching. Books on the atonement do not commonly deal with this topic,

154

for the simple reason that the most obvious impetus for the theology of the atonement derives from the New Testament letters, especially those of St Paul and the letter to the Hebrews. So far, we have only dealt with the kingdom n relation to justification by faith. We have also seen how important are the stories of Jesus' healing miracles to the way the new life is depicted and understood. The kingdom is not an obsolete concept, buried behind the post-Pentecost proclamation of the Church. Indeed, the relationship of the kingdom and the Church is of vital importance to the understanding of both the atonement and evangelism.[12]

In essence, the kingdom is the non-territorial realm where God's sovereignty is acknowledged. It is the person-transforming knowledge of forgiveness, wholeness and freedom. And it is greeted with praise. 'My soul tells out the greatness of the Lord, my spirit has rejoiced in God my Saviour', says Mary (Luke 1:46). 'Praise to the Lord, the God of Israel! For he has turned to his people and set them free', says Zechariah (Luke 1:68). 'Glory to God in highest heaven', says the heavenly host (Luke 2:14). Those who witnessed first the forgiveness, then the healing, of the paralysed man, 'were all lost in amazement and praised God' (Luke 5:26). Praise punctuates the entire gospel of Luke to its end, where the disciples, having received the risen Jesus' final blessing, 'returned to Jerusalem full of joy, and spent all their time in the temple praising God' (Luke 24:52f).

This praise embraces, too, the agony of the passion. Those who saw Jesus die, 'went home beating their breasts' (Luke 23:48). At the Last Supper Jesus refuses the cup, saying he will not drink the fruit of the vine, 'until the time when the kingdom of God comes' (Luke 22:18). We are to understand that his coming sacrificial death prepares the way for the kingdom of God, in the very face of the apparent supremacy of evil.[13] But the kingdom is where the 'cup of blessing' is enjoyed, by virtue of Jesus' acceptance of the cup of suffering.

The Church is to be the sign of God's kingdom, and so to embody the praise of God. The Church has therefore adopted into its worship the texts from the visionary book of Revelation, which record the words of those who stand before the throne of God worshipping him day and night in his temple: 'Worthy is the Lamb who was slain, to receive power and wealth, wisdom and might, honour and glory and praise!' (Rev. 5:12). The Church is thus connected, through its worship, to the eschatological gathering from east and west, north and south, of a vast multitude, not all of whom have been her members. This vital perspective connects the theme of evangelism to our discussion of other faiths. The task of the Church is to be faithful to its commission to preach the Gospel. But it has no concomitant obligation to restrict anticipated participation in God's kingdom to the public membership of the Church. God alone knows what is necessary for a person to be saved. The task of any Christian in relation to any other human being is to share a sense of gratitude to God for his gifts; and both to invite, and be open to be invited, by the other into a deeper enjoyment of the praise of God.

EVANGELISM, COMMITMENT AND SACRIFICE

The theme of praise connects intimately with that of sacrifice through the biblical phrase, 'the sacrifice of praise and thanksgiving' (Ps. 116:17). In itself, that simply refers to the praise of God which accompanies sacrifices. But that praise is anything but perfunctory. A Church brought up on the psalms is embedded in a movement between contrition and praise, between the sacrifice of God, which is 'a broken and contrite heart' (Ps. 51:17), and a longing for God in his sanctuary which bursts out in his praises:

Thus all my life I bless you;
in your name I lift my hands in prayer.
I am satisfied as with a rich feast
and there is a shout of praise on my lips.

(Ps. 63:4–5)

The understanding that the whole of life may be construed as an act of praise, both silent and spoken, commended itself to St Paul ('always be joyful; pray continually; give thanks whatever happens; for this is what God wills for you in Christ Jesus', 1 Thess.5:16–18).

If this were all that was involved, it could be construed as an invitation to a life of unremitting cheerfulness, an exhausting effort always to look on the bright side of things. Exposure to the evil of the world – human wickedness on a scale of the Nazi or Pol Pot regimes, and severe physical or mental suffering – would soon cure us of such superficiality. But the death of Christ invites us to a profounder kind of gratitude – a gratitude able to look without flinching at the very heart of darkness.

'Were you there when they crucified my Lord?' The unselfconscious implication of this profoundly appropriate question has been the explicit theme of this book – namely, that we live inside the narratives of Jesus' way to crucifixion, his death, resurrection and ascension. We were there when they crucified our Lord: we were there as Judas, in petty acts of betrayal; as the other disciples, who at first simply fled but who crept back; as Mary and the other women, who were faithful in their instinct for such life as there was left; as the soldiers, who brutally and casually – or even out of compassion – proposed to finish the matter off; as the centurion, who recognised goodness when he saw it; as the crowd, who impotently beat their breasts at the inhuman awfulness of the act of crucifixion. We were there as Jesus looked with compassion at us, spectator-agents in the myriad guises of evil and weakness, and loved us to the end.

> This is my Friend,
> In whose sweet praise
> I all my days
> Could gladly spend.
>   (S. Crossman, 1624–83, 'My song is love unknown')

We do not see the transaction which that dying accomplishes. We do not hold in our hands the scales of retribution, or measure the weight of the respective forces. But we know intuitively that it has both an external and an internal dimension. By 'external', I mean all that theology reaches for and tries to express in speaking of God's reconciling – at-oning – the world to himself. The unavoidable narrative way of representing that external act is in terms of before and after. Before that death we were enemies; after it we have been made friends. The death was intended, planned and needed; but it was freely, generously, spontaneously offered. In the external forum it is a sacrifice – *the* sacrifice – holy, costly, complete, efficacious. It deals with sin, because it concentrates evil publicly and openly – but is not obliterated by it. It deals with the ambiguities of power, because the sheer destructive energy of human malevolence and weakness proves less powerful than goodness, humility and love.

But it also has an unmistakable internal dimension, which we do not see – though we see its effects. For all who know themselves loved and befriended, even as co-crucifiers, there is a release from fear and impotence and casual malice.[14] That is salvation. It is freedom from the way in which death tyrannises by frightening us into cautious mediocrity; freedom from the way sin worms its way into every aspect of our attitudes and behaviour; and freedom from the vanity and self-regard of conscious moralism. Death, sin and law were identified as the despots; and participation in God's kingdom throws us into the midst of an unrelenting warfare against them and their insidious effects. The offer and reality of the Gospel is to live in freedom from them – not finally free in this life, but confident in the ultimate enjoyment of a richer and fuller personal being.

Evangelism is the invitation, in word and deed, to join what then becomes a fuller chorus of praise.[15] To return to the analogy of singing, it is as if the human voice needed a confident teacher to liberate its potential. The sounds we tentatively make are inhibited by fear. But there is a way of enabling our potential as singers to be liberated – and having been liberated, to be enhanced. To the proper production of the voice there is an external technique to be mastered; but psychological factors are important too. Confidence in our personhood plays a considerable role in overcoming anxiety and inhibition. To sing well requires a delicate combination of self-discipline and self-abandonment.

The atonement is God's work in liberating humanity for the praise of God. Two verses in Psalm 51 speak of this process:

> Deliver me from blood-guiltiness, O God, thou that art
> the God of my health:
> and my tongue shall sing of thy righteousness;
> Thou shalt open my lips, O Lord:
> and my mouth shall shew thy praise.
>
> (Ps. 51:14–15) Coverdale, BCP

Evangelising is the process of issuing an attractive invitation to a life made up of praise in every part.[16] It is motivated by a desire that the chorus shall grow, that men and women shall transformingly belong to the vast company of those who offer themselves, their souls and bodies, as a living sacrifice to God in gratitude for the generosity of his grace, and be transformed by that belonging.

EPILOGUE

Praise II

King of Glory, King of Peace,
    I will love thee:
And that love may never cease,
    I will move thee.

Thou hast granted my request,
    Thou hast heard me:
Thou didst note my working breast,
    Thou hast spared me.

Wherefore with my utmost art
    I will sing thee,
And the cream of all my heart
    I will bring thee.

Though my sins against me cried,
    Thou didst clear me;
And alone, when they replied,
    Thou didst hear me.

Sev'n whole days, not one in seven,
    I will praise thee

Epilogue

In my heart though not in heaven,
    I can raise thee.

Thou grew'st soft and moist with tears,
    Thou relentedst:
And when justice called for fears,
    Thou dissentedst.

Small it is, in this poor sort
    To enrol thee:
Ev'n eternity's too short
    To extol thee.

George Herbert

NOTES

∞∞∞∞∞∞∞

CHAPTER 1: What is atonement?

1. These are the familiar words in many liturgies. The sentence is, however, composite, see Matt. 26:28 and 1 Cor. 11:25.

2. *Oxford English Dictionary* (Oxford, 1989), vol. 1, pp.754–5.

3. C.E.B. Cranfield, *The Epistle to the Romans*, vol. 1 (6th edn, Edinburgh, 1975), p.255.

4. See the copious literature documented by C.D. Hancock, *The Priesthood of Christ in Anglican Doctrine and Devotion, 1827–1900*, unpublished PhD thesis, University of Durham, 1985.

5. The basic thesis of the book, which was that the theology of the early church was to be preferred to medieval theology, greatly appealed to the Anglican translator, Father A.G. Hebert. Hebert was a liturgical scholar with a critical attitude towards the medieval liturgical inheritance, but who did not want to cut himself off from the tradition. His Anglican-sounding verdict on Aulén's book was that it presented a view of atonement 'at once truly evangelical and truly Catholic'; Gustaf Aulén, *Christus Victor* (trans. A.G. Hebert, London 1931; original in Swedish, 1930), Preface, pp.x–xi.

6. *Ibid.*, pp.174–5.

7. O.C. Quick, *Doctrines of the Creed* (London 1938).

8. T.H. Hughes, *The Atonement: Modern Theories of the Doctrine* (London 1949).

9. H.A. Hodges, *The Pattern of Atonement* (London 1955).

10. F.W. Dillistone, *The Christian Understanding of Atonement* (London 1968), p.27.

11. Anselm of Canterbury, *Why God became Man* (trans. E.R. Fairweather, Library of Christian Classics X; London, 1956).

12. See F.L. Horton, *The Melchizedek Tradition* (Cambridge 1976).

163

13. The deeper background to this emphasis on narrative is explored in Hans Frei, *Theology and Narrative* (Oxford, 1993).

14. Louis Allen, *John Henry Newman and the Abbé Jager: A Controversy on Scripture and Tradition* (London 1975) pp.89f.

15. *Ibid.*, p.89.

16. See E.P. Sanders, *Jesus and Judaism* (London 1985), pp.294–318 on the evidence for the trial and crucifixion of Jesus.

17. J. Jeremias, *Der Opfertod Jesu Christi* (Stuttgart, 1963).

18. There is a good treatment of metaphor and atonement in C.E. Gunton, *The Actuality of Atonement* (Edinburgh 1988).

19. Well put by R.C. Moberly in his classic work, *Atonement and Personality* (London 1901) pp.341f.

20. George Herbert (1593–1633), poet and priest; his poems under the title *The Temple*, were published posthumously in 1633.

21. S. Toulmin, *Cosmopolis: The Hidden Agenda of Modernity* (New York, 1990); and J.-F. Lyotard, *The Post-Modern Condition: A Report on Knowledge* (English translation, Manchester 1984).

22. W. Brueggemann, *The Bible and Post-Modern Imagination: Texts under Negotiation* (London 1993) pp.20 and 61f.

INTERLUDE: Justifying the ways of God in Milton's *Paradise Lost*

1. Text in F. Carey and A. Fowler (eds), *The Poems of John Milton* (London, 1968) and *The Complete English Poems/John Milton*, edited and introduced by Gordon Campbell (London 4th edn, 1992). The Carey-Fowler text is used here.

2. A major contemporary proponent of the 'free-will defence' is Alvin Plantinga, *The Nature of Necessity* (Oxford, 1974), pp.170–1, 184. The point is discussed by D.R. Danielson in *Milton's Good God, A Study in Literary Theodicy* (Cambridge 1982), ch.4.

3. Discussion in P.T. Geach, *Providence and Evil* (Cambridge 1977), pp.3, 28.

4. Very thoroughly expounded in D.R. Danielson, *Milton's Good God*, ch.3.

5. See *Cur Deus Homo* (*Why God became Man*), chs 12 and 21.

6. Cited from John Donne's *Sermons*, Vol 8, p.207, by C.A. Patrides, *Milton and the Christian Tradition* (Oxford 1966), p.139.

7. H. Blaimires, *Milton's Creation, A Guide through Paradise Lost* (London 1971) p.72.

Notes

CHAPTER 2: Justification by faith

1. The posthumously published 'Learned discourse of justification, works, and how the foundation of faith is overthrown' (preached in 1586; published 1612; critical text in W. Speed Hill (ed.), *The Folger Library Edition of the Works of Richard Hooker*, vol. 5 *Tractates and Sermons* (Cambridge MA 1990), pp.105–69).

2. See C. Blakemore, *Mechanics of the Mind* (Cambridge, 1977) pp.1–27.

3. L. Gormally (ed), *Euthanasia: Clinical Practice and the Law* (London 1994).

4. And note: 'We cannot tamper with the revelation of original sin without undermining the mystery of Christ', *Catechism of the Catholic Church* (English translation, Dublin, 1994) p.87.

5. Wisdom of Solomon 14:25f; 4 Macc. 1:26f; Philo, *Sac* 32; 1 Clem. 35:5; *Did.* 2–5; Barn. 18–20. See W. Meeks, *The Origins of Christian Morality: The First Two Centuries* (New Haven 1993), pp.121–9.

6. See William Stafford, *Disordered Loves, Healing the Seven Deadly Sins* (Cowley 1994).

7. 'Thou that hast giv'n so much to me,
   Give one thing more, a grateful heart.
   Not thankful, when it pleaseth me;
   As if thy blessing had spare days:
   But such a heart, whose pulse may be thy praise.'
   (George Herbert, 'Gratefulness')

8. See J.I. Packer, 'What did the cross achieve?', *Tyndale Bulletin*, 25 (1974), pp.3–45.

9. See E.P. Sanders, *Paul and Palestinian Judaism* (London 1977), pp.431–542; and the Lutheran New Testament scholar, J. Reumann, *Righteousness in the New Testament* (Philadelphia, 1982), pp.41–123.

10. J. Riches, *Jesus and the Transformation of Judaism* (London 1980), p.140.

11. Discussed in E.P. Sanders, *Jesus*, pp.61–76.

12. Raymond Brown, *An Introduction to New Testament Christology* (London 1994) ch.7.

13. See M. Hengel, *The Atonement, a Study of the Origins of the Doctrine in the New Testament* (London 1981).

14. Eirenically presented and discussed by George Tavard, *Justification, an Ecumenical Study* (New York 1983), ch.3.
15. See the able summary of the dispute on A.E. McGrath, *Iustitia Dei, A History of the Christian Doctrine of Justification* vol. 2 (Cambridge 1986), pp.1–21.
16. For what follows see R.W. Jenson, *Unbaptised God: the Basic Flaw in Ecumenical Theology* (Minneapolis 1992).
17. H.G. Anderson, T.A. Murphy and J.A. Burgess (eds), *Justification by Faith: Lutherans and Catholics in Dialogue*, vol. 7 (Minneapolis 1985).
18. See the following reports of the Lutheran-Roman Catholic Joint Commission: *Justification by Faith* (1985), *The Condemnations of the Reformation Era – Do They Still Divide?* (1986) and *Church and Justification* (1994); all published by The Lutheran World Federation and the Pontifical Council for Promoting Christian Unity.

CHAPTER 3: Merit and reward

1. Treated with profundity by Hans W. Frei, *The Identity of Jesus Christ: the Hermeneutical Basis of Dogmatic Theology* (Philadelphia 1975).
2. See E. Leach, *Social Anthropology* (London 1982), ch.5.
3. R. Strier, *Love Known: theology and experience in George Herbert's poetry* (Chicago 1983), p.80.
4. See 'Love bade me welcome', Stephen Sykes, *Unashamed Anglicanism* (London 1995), pp.49–63.
5. G. Rupp, *Religion in England 1688–1791* (Oxford 1986), pp.280–1.
6. In the Old Testament we have the following passages: Ps. 62:12; Prov. 23:12; Eccles. 12:14; Isa. 3.10f; Jer. 17:10; Hos 12:2. In the New Testament: Matt. 7:21; 16:27; 25:31–46; John 5:28f; 2 Cor 5:10; 11:15b; Gal. 6:7–9; Eph. 6:8; Col. 3:24f; 2 Tim. 4:14; 1 Pet. 1:17; Rev. 2:23; 20:12f; 22:12.
7. On which see E.P. Sanders, *Paul and Palestinian Judaism* (London 1977), pp.516f.
8. Newman caricatured Luther's doctrine of justification by faith in this way in his 1837 *Lectures on Justification*. See A.E. McGrath, *Iustitia Dei*, vol. 2, (Cambridge 1986), pp.121–30.
9. 'Faith' and 'revelation' are correlative terms in Christian theology. See S.W. Sykes, 'Faith', in G. Wainwright (ed.), *Keeping the Faith* (London 1988), pp.1–24.

10. ARCIC II, *Salvation and the Church* (1986), para. 15.
11. Prayer of thanksgiving, after communion, 1662 Book of Common Prayer. See also the words, 'That all our doings may be ordered by thy governance, to do always what is righteous in thy sight' (third collect, Morning Prayer).
12. Brilliantly explored in George Herbert's 'The Thanksgiving'.

CHAPTER 4: Salvation and other faiths

1. Hick, 'Jesus and the World Religions', in J. Hick (ed.), *The Myth of God Incarnate* (London 1977), p.181.
2. S.J. Samartha (ed.), *Living Faiths and the Ecumenical Movement* (Geneva 1971); S.J. Samartha and J.B. Taylor, *Christian-Muslim Dialogue* (Geneva 1973); S.J. Samartha, *Living Faiths and Ultimate Goals; a Continuing Dialogue* (Geneva 1974); *Courage for Dialogue, Ecumenical issues in Inter-Religious Relationships* (Geneva 1981); *One Christ – Many Religions: towards a revised Christology* (Maryknoll 1991).
3. Vatican II, *Lumen Gentium*, ch.2, section 16 (trans. and ed. W.A. Abbott London/Dublin 1966), p.35.
4. See W. Ariarajah, *Hindus and Christians: a century of Protestant ecumenical thought* (Grand Rapids 1991) pp.17–31.
5. F.D.E. Schleiermacher, *On Religion: Speeches to its Cultured Despisers* (trans. R. Crouter, Cambridge 1988; first German edn, 1799).
6. Cited by the distinguished Jesuit theologian, Y.M. Congar, in *The Wide World, My Parish* (London, 1961; original French n.d.), p.95. Fulgentius (*c.* 468–533) was a North African monk and a disciple of St Augustine.
7. *Ibid.*, p.102.
8. G. D'Costa, *Theology and Religious Pluralism* (Oxford 1986), pp.7–9.
9. J. Farquhar, *The Crown of Hinduism* (London 1913). See, for example, p.132: 'Christ thus crowns the Hindu family with a structure which is new, yet is in no sense alien, but is the natural consummation of the older and less perfect system'.
10. R. Panikkar, *The Unknown Christ of Hinduism: Towards an Ecumenical Christophany* (rev. edn, London 1981).
11. *The Mystery of Salvation, the Story of God's Gift* (London 1995), p.171.
12. Indignantly reported by Bishop J.W. Colenso in his *Ten Weeks in Natal* (Cambridge 1855), pp.252f and in *St Paul's Epistle to the*

Notes

Romans: New Translated and Explained from a Missionary Point of View (Cambridge 1861), p.211. See also G.W. Cox, *The Life of John William Colenso* (London 1880), vol. 1, p.154.

13. *The Mystery of Salvation* (see footnote 11), p.161.
14. J. Sanders, *No Other Name: Can only Christians be Saved?* (London 1994) gives an able account and critique of those who have held and hold the view that all the unevangelised are damned, pp.37–79.
15. See W.A. Meeks, *The Origins of Christian Morality* ch.10, referring to F. Kermode, *The Sense of an Ending: Studies in the Theory of Fiction* (Oxford 1968).
16. Citing Ezekiel 18:23.
17. Luther on the First Commandment, 16–17 *The Greater Catechism* (trans. in T.G. Tappert (ed.), *The Book of Concord* (Philadelphia 1959), pp.366–7.
18. H.R. Niebuhr, *The Meaning of Revelation* (New York 1941), p.77.
19. This view is often called indifferentism and is specifically condemned in Article 18, 'Of obtaining eternal Salvation only by the name of Christ', of the Church of England's Thirty-nine Articles.

INTERLUDE: The parable of the ring in Lessing's *Nathan the Wise*

1. The different types of relativism are distinguished with great skill by S. Coakley in *Christ without Absolutes: a study of the Christology of Ernst Troeltsch* (Oxford 1988).
2. See F. Niewöhner, *Veritas sive Varietas, Lessings Toleranzparabel und das Buch Von den drei Betrügern* (Heidelberg 1988).
3. This, and subsequent quotations, are from *Nathan the Wise* (trans. S. Clennel and R. Philip (Milton Keynes 1992)).

CHAPTER 5: The sacraments and last things

1. R.C. Moberly, *Atonement and Personality* (London 1901), p.151.
2. P.T. Forsyth, *Lectures on the Church and the Sacraments* (London 1917), p.40.
3. W. Meeks, *The First Urban Christians, The Social World of the Apostle Paul* (New Haven 1983), p.88.
4. M. Fortes, *Religion, Morality and the Person* (Cambridge 1987), p.4.

5. M. Douglas, *Natural Symbols* (London 1970) p.25.
6. *Ibid.*, p.28
7. *Ibid.*, p.27f.
8. E. Duffy, *The Stripping of the Altars*, (New Haven 1992).
9. Augustine of Hippo, *The City of God*, vol.10, 6, 1 (trans. H. Bettenson, Penguin Books, Harmondsworth 1972, p.379).
10. See the argument on this point between myself and I.U. Dalferth, in S.W. Sykes (ed. *Sacrifice and Redemption* (Cambridge 1991), pp.282–325.
11. H. Gese, *Essays on Biblical Theology* (Minneapolis 1981), pp.117–40.
12. A.N. Chester, 'Hebrews: the final sacrifice', in Sykes (ed. *Sacrifice and Redemption*, pp.57–72.
13. M. Hengel, *The Atonement*, p.72; also printed in *The Cross of the Son of God* (London, 1986), p.260.
14. A history and wholehearted defence of the use of sacrifice in theology is to be found in I. Bradley, *The Power of Sacrifice* (London 1995).
15. E. Leach, *Culture and Communication* (Cambridge 1976) pp.81–93.
16. G. Every, *The Baptismal Sacrifice* (London 1959).
17. *On the City of God*, vol.10, 20 (Bettenson p.401).
18. M.D. Hooker, *From Adam to Christ, Essays on Paul* (Cambridge 1990), chs 1–4.
19. D. Rensberger, *Overcoming the World, Politics and Community in the Gospel of John* (London 1988), p.81.
20. See S.W. Sykes, 'Life after Death: the Christian Doctrine of Heaven' in R.W.A. McKinney (ed.), *Creation, Christ and Culture: Studies in Honour of T.F. Torrance* (Edinburgh 1976), pp.250–71.
21. R. Brown, Appendix II, 'The reality of the resurrection of Jesus', in *An Introduction to New Testament Christology* (London 1994), pp.162–170.

CHAPTER 6: A theology of evangelism

1. Karen Blixen published 'Babette's Feast' under the pseudonym of I. Dinesen, *Anecdotes of Destiny* (reprinted, London 1958), pp.23–68.
2. W. Meeks, *The Origins of Christian Morality*, ch.2: 'Turning: Moral Consequences of Conversion', starts with the Thessalonian church. Citations from pp.31 and 36.

3. P.K. Stevenson, 'Rehabilitating Judgement. The Case for a Neglected Doctrine', M. Litt thesis, University of Birmingham, 1994.

4. R.E. Brown, *The Letters of John*, (London 1983), pp.542–53.

5. Rensberger, p.130.

6. See above: ch.4, note 12.

7. A.J. Arberry, *Sufism. An Account of the Mystics of Islam* (London 1950), pp.42f.

8. 'There is a choice: good or evil', *The Spectator*, 18 April 1992.

9. J. McLeod Campbell, *The Nature of the Atonement, and its Relation to Remission of Sins and Eternal Life* (4th edn; London 1959).

10. Michael Walzer, *Thick and Thin, The Moral Argument at Home and Abroad* (Notre Dame 1994).

11. W. Brueggemann makes explicit the importance of connecting praise to liberation, in *Israel's Praises* (Philadelphia 1988).

12. William Abraham, *The Logic of Evangelism* (London 1989), defines evangelism as a polymorphous activity governed by the goad of initiating people into the kingdom of God.

13. M. Hengel, *The Atonement*, p.72.

14. 'The spring of evil becomes conscious and personal in the face of the Crucified, as we know our worst, and know, for the first time, a total acceptance', Sebastian Moore, *The Crucified is no Stranger* (New York 1977). This remarkable book is a profound exploration of transformation through the discovery of God's love.

15. See also Stephen Sykes, 'An Anglican theology of evangelism' in *Unashamed Anglicanism* (London 1995), pp.201–10.

16. 'Fill thou my life, O Lord my God/In every part with praise'; H. Bonar (1808–89).

Name and Subject Index

The subject indexing is necessarily selective, and several key theological terms are referred to pervasively in the text and are only indexed where there is significant direct discussion. References to endnotes (selectively indexed) are to the page on which the note's text appears.

Index of Biblical References

Name and Subject Index